1980

A CLINICAL AND EDUCATIONAL MANUAL
for use with
THE UZGIRIS AND HUNT SCALES OF INFANT PSYCHOLOGICAL DEVELOPMENT

A CLINICAL AND EDUCATIONAL MANUAL
for use with
THE UZGIRIS AND HUNT SCALES OF INFANT PSYCHOLOGICAL DEVELOPMENT

by
Carl J. Dunst
Department of Special Education
College of Education
Division of Human and Community Resources
University of Maryland, College Park

University Park Press
Baltimore

UNIVERSITY PARK PRESS
International Publishers in Science, Medicine, and Education
233 East Redwood Street
Baltimore, Maryland 21202

Composed by University Park Press, Typesetting Division.
Manufactured in the United States of America by
Collins Lithographing and Printing Co., Inc.

Library of Congress Cataloging in Publication Data
Dunst, Carl J
A clinical and educational manual for use with the Uzgiris and Hunt scales
of infant psychological development.
Bibliography: p. 57
Includes index.
1. Psychological tests for children. 2. Infant psychology. I. Title. [DNLM: 1. Child development. 2. Child
psychology. 3. Psychological tests—In infancy and childhood. WS105.5.E8 D926c]
BF722.D86   155.4'13'0287   80-131
ISBN 0-8391-1571-7

This manual is designed to be used clinically in conjunction with *Assessment in Infancy: Ordinal Scales
of Psychological Development,* by Profs. Ina Uzgiris and J. McVicker Hunt (University of Illinois Press,
1975), and therefore develops information contained in that text. Kind acknowledgment and credit are
extended to the University of Illinois Press and Profs. Uzgiris and Hunt; however, publication of this
manual does not imply endorsement by either the publisher or the authors.

Contents

Preface

A quarter of a century has passed since Jean Piaget's trilogy on infant development was translated into English. The descriptions of the genesis of infant intelligence that Piaget presents in these three volumes have served the useful purpose of providing a framework for the design of sensorimotor scales of infant psychological development. Ina Uzgiris, J. McVicker Hunt, Sibylle Escalona, Harvey Corman, Irene Casati, and Irene Lezine among others have been leaders in the development of these Piagetian-based infant assessment scales. The construction of these scales coincided with an upsurge in the number of empirical investigations designed to identify the structure and composition of infant intelligence. The bulk of the available evidence indicates that, rather than being a unitary, monolithic trait, infant intelligence is comprised of multiple and varied sets of abilities and that there are qualitative shifts in the prominence of these distinct factors at different levels of development (Dunst, 1978).

Piagetian, or ordinal, infant scales, as they have come to be called, reflect quite accurately this conceptualization of infant intelligence—both theoretically and organizationally. At the theoretical level, Piaget considers the genesis of infant intelligence to represent qualitative reorganizations of sensorimotor schemes (structures) at successive levels of development. Organizationally, Piagetian infant scales include a number of separate scales or branches of development (e.g., object permanence, vocal imitation, play, and causality) in which the achievements comprising the content of each domain are intended to measure the types of reorganizations that occur in the development of these particular concepts or constructs.

Although the developers of Piagetian-based infant scales have recognized the potential utility of their assessment instruments for clinical and educational purposes, there do not currently exist either procedures that clinicians and other individuals can use to determine an individual's *overall* pattern of sensorimotor development or guidelines that can be used for the design of psychoeducational intervention activities. This manual is designed specifically to accomplish these tasks. Herein is described an approach that uses the Uzgiris and Hunt (1975) scales of infant psychological development for clinical and educational purposes. The strategy presented is intended to serve as an alternative to the traditional, psychometric approach to infant assessment.

This manual is divided into four major sections. The introductory section presents an overview of the major characteristics of ordinal-based infant scales, describes some basic similarities and differences between Piagetian and psychometric infant tests, and briefly reviews the data that lend credibility to the use of ordinal scales with retarded and handicapped populations. Also, the clinical-educational process that is delineated in the three subsequent sections of the manual is introduced.

The clinical-educational process that is described in this manual is designed to yield information concerning three aspects of a child's sensorimotor development: quantitative characteristics, qualitative characteristics, and information useful for the design of psychoeducational intervention procedures. Procedures used to describe a child's sensorimotor performance in *quantitative* terms were specifically developed for this manual. Preliminary data indicate that the procedures appear to have excellent concurrent validity with regard to predicting actual psychometric test performance. However, more in-depth investigations are clearly needed before the procedures can be accepted as truly valid for determining the quantitative aspects of sensorimotor performance. Such investigations are currently underway.

The description of the child's sensorimotor performance in *qualitative* terms represents the critical and most important step in the overall clinical-educational process. Procedures used to describe a child's performance in qualitative terms permit an assessment of the extent to which a child is delayed in development, whether or not a child's pattern of development is typical or atypical, a determination of a child's major strengths and weaknesses, and an identification of appropriate interventions designed to remediate or ameliorate any delays and/or deficits found.

Section Two describes the clinical record forms developed for this manual. Each of the major record form sections are described, their utility is discussed, and illustrative examples of their use are presented. Section Three describes the clinical directions used in administration of the scales, and presents the scoring procedures used to determine a child's level of sensorimotor performance in each of the branches of development comprising the content of the Uzgiris and Hunt assessment instrument.

Section Four of the manual describes the procedures used for recording a child's sensorimotor abilities, constructing a profile of sensorimotor abilities, and interpreting the results. Also, guidelines and a model that can serve as a framework for the design of individualized psychoeducational intervention activities are presented. Eleven case studies of both nonhandicapped and handicapped children are presented to illustrate the procedures used in recording, profiling, interpreting, and utilizing the results of an assessment.

This manual was written to maximize the utility of the Uzgiris and Hunt scales when used for clinical and educational purposes. If the user of this manual finds that the procedures described lead to additional insights concerning a child's sensorimotor capabilities and aid in the design of intervention activities, the goal that I set for myself will have been attained.

REFERENCES

Dunst, C. J. The structure of infant intelligence: An historical overview. *Intelligence*, 1978, 2, 321–331.

Uzgiris, I., and Hunt, J. McV. *Assessment in infancy: Ordinal scales of psychological development.* Urbana: University of Illinois Press, 1975.

Acknowledgments

I would like to take this opportunity to express my appreciation and gratitude to all those individuals who have been involved in the various phases of the development of this manual. I am indebted to Dr. Harris Gabel, who initially encouraged me to consider writing this manual. Special thanks are extended to Paula Goodroe, Director of the John F. Kennedy Center Experimental School, George Peabody College, who supported the development of this manual, and to her Infant Unit staff, Mary Porter, Jennifer Hamilton, and Nancy Wallace, who provided me with valuable comments and suggestions concerning the clinical record forms and directions for administration developed for this manual. I am especially grateful to Dr. Ina Uzgiris and Dr. J. McVicker Hunt for their helpful comments, suggestions, and criticisms. However, their endorsement of this manual should not be inferred. Permission from the University of Illinois Press to utilize information from Uzgiris and Hunt's book is appreciated. I am additionally indebted to Valarie Dunst, who typed various versions of this manual, and to Janet Hankin of University Park Press, who was instrumental in facilitating the review and publication of this manual, and to Megan Shelton of University Park Press, who did a superb job of editing the manuscript. Above all, I wish to thank the parents and children who participated in the testing phase of the development of this manual.

The initial preparation of this manual was supported, in part, by Grant 5 T32 HD07045 from the National Institute of Child Health and Human Development to the John F. Kennedy Center, George Peabody College, Nashville, Tennessee.

To my son Kerry.

A CLINICAL AND EDUCATIONAL MANUAL
for use with
THE UZGIRIS AND HUNT SCALES OF INFANT PSYCHOLOGICAL DEVELOPMENT

INTRODUCTION

This manual describes an approach for the clinical and educational use of the Uzgiris and Hunt (1975) scales of sensorimotor development. This assessment instrument "... permits new ways of assessing the level of development in individual infants, new ways of comparing the levels of cognitive organization achieved by different infants, and a way of determining the influence of various constellations of environmental circumstances on early development" (Uzgiris & Hunt, 1975, p. ix). This manual is intended to be used to assess the development of infants and older retarded and handicapped children who are at risk for manifesting delays and/or deviations in their sensorimotor development.

Unlike traditional infant tests, which measure global aspects of overall cognitive performance, the Uzgiris and Hunt scales assess an individual's level of sensorimotor development in seven structurally related branches: I—Visual Pursuit and the Permanence of Object, II—Means for Obtaining Desired Environmental Events, IIIA—The Development of Vocal Imitation, IIIB—The Development of Gestural Imitation, IV—The Development of Operational Causality, V—The Construction of Object Relations in Space, and VI—The Development of Schemes for Relating to Objects. These seven branches parallel the domains of sensorimotor development delineated by Piaget (1936, 1937, 1945). Achievements comprising the content of each branch of development are considered to be particular aspects of a more general process involved in the genesis of sensorimotor (i.e., practical adaptive) intelligence. Moreover, development in each of the sensorimotor branches emerges through the same six-stage sequence that was posited by Piaget (1936). Selected characteristics of the attainments for the separate branches of development at each of the six sequential stages of the sensorimotor period are presented in Table 1. These descriptions are adapted from Piaget's (1936, 1937, 1945) own accounts of the development of sensorimotor intelligence.

One characteristic of the Uzgiris and Hunt scales that makes them different from traditional infant tests is their ordinal construction. Each of the successive items on the individual scales of sensorimotor development constitutes a hierarchical sequence. In other words, the landmarks on each of the scales are sequential levels in the genesis of a particular construct or concept (e.g., object permanence). Moreover, the successive levels of achievements "... at the higher levels do not incidentally follow, but are intrinsically derived from those at the preceding level and encompass them within the higher levels" (Uzgiris & Hunt, 1975, p. 11). This conceptualization of development considers the acquisition of skill attainments at the lower levels essential for acquiring subsequent cognitive achievements.

Because of the ordinal construction of the scales, it is possible to ascertain a child's level of cognitive performance by noting the highest item passed on each of the seven scales. Moreover, since development in any one sensorimotor branch is generally unrelated to performance in the other structurally parallel branches of development (Kopp, Sigman, & Parmelee, 1974; Uzgiris, 1973, 1976a), it is possible to discern a child's major strengths and weaknesses by constructing a profile of sensorimotor abilities. Since assessing developmental status is fundamental in clinical work, the clinician should find a profile of abilities advantageous for gauging the extent to which an individual child is advanced or retarded in his or her development. More importantly, because the Uzgiris and Hunt scales assess development in separate branches, the clinician is able to describe the child's sensorimotor capabilities in concrete and specific terms for each individual sensorimotor area.

Besides their utility in clinical use, the educational interventionist should find the information obtained from administration of the Uzgiris and Hunt scales useful for identifying the particular types of experiences that would be most conducive to fostering cog-

Table 1. Selected characteristics of the attainments of the sensorimotor period

Stages (age in months)	Domains of sensorimotor development						
	Purposeful problem solving	Object permanence	Spatial relationships	Causality	Vocal imitation	Gestural imitation	Play[a]
I Use of reflexes (0–1)	Shows only reflexive reactions in response to external stimuli	No active search for objects vanishing from sight	No signs of appreciation of spatial relationships between objects	No signs of understanding causal relationships	Vocal contagion: cries on hearing another infant cry	No signs of imitation of movements he/she performs	No signs of intentional play behavior
II Primary circular reactions (1–4)	First acquired adaptations, coordination of two behavioral schemes (e.g., hand-mouth coordination)	Attempts to maintain visual contact with objects moving outside the visual field	Reacts to external stimuli as representing independent spatial fields (e.g., visual, auditory) rather than as a spatial nexus	Shows signs of precausal understanding (e.g., places thumb in the mouth to suck on it)	Repeats sound just produced following adult imitation of the sound	Repeats movements just made following adult imitation of the action	Produces primary circular reactions repeatedly in an enjoyable manner
III Secondary circular reactions (4–8)	Procedures for making interesting sights last: repeats actions to maintain the reinforcing consequences produced by the action	Reinstates visual contact with objects by (a) anticipating the terminal position of a moving object, and (b) removing a cloth placed over his/her face. Retrieves a partially hidden object	Shows signs of understanding relationships between self and external events (e.g., follows trajectory of rapidly falling objects)	Uses "phenomenalistic procedures" (e.g., generalized excitement) as a causal action to have an adult repeat an interesting spectacle	Imitates sounds already in his/her repertoire	Imitates simple gestures already in his/her repertoire that are *visible* to self	Repetition of interesting actions applied to familiar objects
IV Coordination of secondary circular reactions (8–12)	Serializes two heretofore separate behaviors in goal-directed sequences	Secures objects *seen* hidden under, behind, etc. a single barrier	Rotates and examines objects with signs of appreciation of their three-dimensional attributes, size, shape, weight, etc.	Touches adult's hands to have that person instigate or continue an interesting game or action	Imitates novel sounds but only ones that are similar to those he/she already produces	Imitates (a) self-movements that are *invisible* (e.g., sticking out the tongue), and (b) novel movements comprised of actions familiar to self	During problem solving sequences, he/she abandons the terminus in favor of playing with the means. Ritualization: applies appropriate social actions to different objects
V Tertiary circular reactions (12–18)	Discovers "novel" means behavior needed to obtain a desired goal	Secures objects hidden through a series of *visible* displacements	Combines and relates objects in different spatial configurations (e.g., places blocks into a cup)	Hands an object to an adult to have that person repeat or instigate a desired action	Imitates novel sound patterns and words that he/she has not previously heard	Imitates novel movements that he/she cannot see self perform (i.e., *invisible* gestures) and that he/she has not previously performed	Adaptative play: begins to use one object (e.g., doll cup) as a substitute for another (e.g., adult-size cup) during play with objects
VI Representation and foresight (18–24)	"Invents" means behavior, via internal thought processes, needed to obtain a desired goal	Recreates sequence of displacements to secure objects: secures objects hidden through a sequence of *invisible* displacements	Manifests the ability to "represent" the nature of spatial relationships that exist between objects, and between objects and self	Shows capacity to (a) infer a cause, given only its effect, and (b) foresee an effect, given a cause	Imitates complex verbalizations. Reproduces previously heard sounds and words from memory; deferred imitation	Imitates complex motor movements. Reproduces previously observed actions from memory; deferred imitation	Symbolic play: uses one object as a "signifier" for another (e.g., a box for a doll bed). Symbolically enacts an event without having ordinarily used objects present

[a]The Schemes for Relating to Objects scale on the Uzgiris and Hunt assessment instrument parallels the achievements of the Play domain as explicated by Piaget (1945).

nitive growth. Hunt (1961, 1963, 1966) describes the procedure whereby assessment results are used to determine educationally relevant experiences as the "problem of the match." This is simply a restatement of the axiom that "learning must start where the learner is." The results of administration of the Uzgiris and Hunt scales can help to identify where the learner "is," and thus provide a reference point for developing and implementing relevant psychoeducational intervention activities.

Before describing the clinical process and record forms developed for use with the Uzgiris and Hunt scales, several important issues should be addressed. First, a few points need to be made regarding some basic similarities and differences in the procedures and objectives used in administering and scoring traditional infant psychometric tests and ordinal infant scales. This is necessary if the utility of ordinal scales is to be fully appreciated. Second, the available data pertaining to the ordinality of sensorimotor development among handicapped populations need to be reviewed. This is necessary before the use of the Uzgiris and Hunt scales with children who have diverse handicapping conditions can be justified.

SIMILARITIES AND DIFFERENCES BETWEEN TRADITIONAL AND ORDINAL INFANT SCALES[1]

The one major similarity between the psychometric and ordinal approaches to infant assessment is the goal of establishing an individual's current developmental status. Using traditional infant tests, this is usually done by determining a child's mental age equivalent (MAE) based on his or her overall test performance. MAEs are ascertained by first determining the total number of items passed, and then finding the average age that corresponds to that particular raw score.

Establishing developmental status using ordinal scales is accomplished by noting the highest item passed on each of the sensorimotor scales administered. Because of their ordinal construction, the highest landmark achieved specifies the particular point along a de-

velopmental continuum (e.g., the genesis of operational causality) at which the child is functioning. Rather than using an MAE, both estimated developmental ages (EDAs) and stage placements for the individual sequential landmarks are used to ascertain a child's performance in the different branches of development.

A second similarity between traditional and ordinal scales concerns the goal of determining a child's developmental strengths and weaknesses. Using traditional infant tests, determining a child's major strengths and weaknesses generally requires "sorting" out those items passed and failed among all the items administered. Conversely, using ordinal scales an individual's strengths and weaknesses are determined by noting in which domain(s) performance is most advanced and in which domain(s) performance is most retarded. Moreover, the profile of abilities constructed from the data obtained from the administration of the Uzgiris and Hunt scales provides a basis for graphically depicting a child's variability in performance across the seven branches of development.

One difference between traditional and ordinal infant scales concerns the nature of the test instruments themselves. In administering traditional infant tests, a child's performance generally extends over items 3 or more months apart. This is due, in part, to the additive conceptualization of development underlying these tests (see Uzgiris & Hunt, 1975, chapter 2). Because of this, establishing basal and ceiling performance is a common practice. The basal level is the chronological age corresponding to the item preceding the first failure, whereas the ceiling level is the chronological age corresponding to the item represented by the highest item passed. Ordinal scales yield only ceiling performance because of their hierarchical construction. The highest item passed on each scale determines ceiling performance. This is the point at which all subsequent landmarks on a particular scale are not manifested in response to the assessment procedures.

A second major difference between ordinal and traditional infant scales concerns general administration procedures and the test materials used to assess developmental performance. Nearly all psychometric tests have both standard test procedures and standardized materials that must be used in the administration of the scales. Instructions almost always specify that the standardized procedures must be followed rigidly, and that the examiner is not per-

---

[1]The discussion of the similarities and differences between traditional and ordinal infant scales presented here is restricted to practical considerations. Theoretical differences between psychometric and ordinal infant scales are discussed by Uzgiris and Hunt (1975) in their monograph.

mitted to alter the directions in any way. Thus, although a test behavior may be manifested in response to other than the test materials, generally such behaviors cannot be used in scoring the tests unless the instructions indicate that they may.

The test procedures suggested for administering ordinal scales are generally much more flexible, and permit the examiner to use both varied materials and eliciting situations to determine performance in each domain. Furthermore, particularly on the schemes for relating to objects, vocal imitation, and gestural imitation scales, spontaneously emitted behaviors can be used to ascertain a child's sensorimotor abilities. In using traditional infant tests, the examiner is assessing an individual's responses to standardized procedures and materials, whereas, when using ordinal scales, the examiner's role is eliciting optimal performance in each domain using a variety of assessment procedures and materials.

A final distinction between ordinal and traditional infant tests concerns the outcome data that are obtained. Traditional infant scales generally yield either a developmental quotient (DQ) or an intelligence quotient (IQ). These summary indices, computed either as a ratio between a child's MAE and chronological age or as a deviation score, are intended to provide a measure of differential rate of development. In determining a child's relative developmental standing, the individual's DQ or IQ is compared to standardized norms, thus providing a basis for noting the extent to which the child deviates from normal development.

Ordinal scales yield no DQ or IQ scores, and therefore comparisons to standardized norms are not possible. However, the extent to which a child is advanced or retarded in development can be gauged by comparing the child's chronological age with the EDA placement corresponding to the highest item passed on each of the seven scales. Consequently, it is possible to ascertain a child's developmental standing by noting the difference between the child's chronological age and the EDA placement corresponding to the highest item passed on each scale. These differences or deviation scores are intended to provide a measure of the extent to which delays and/or discrepancies are present. Assessing developmental performance in this manner provides the clinician with information that should prove much more beneficial in making statements concerning the *relative* developmental standing of a child for individual scales

rather than for overall performance (although the latter can also be determined—see Appendix D).

CHARACTERISTICS OF SENSORIMOTOR DEVELOPMENT AMONG HANDICAPPED CHILDREN

The majority of studies on sensorimotor development have been directed toward determining whether infants (nonhandicapped and handicapped) acquire particular postulated sequences of behavior in the stage order posited by Piaget (1936). The principle statistical procedure used to assess the stage progression hypothesis has been Green's (1956) version of Guttman's (1950) method for scaling patterns of responses. The procedure, termed scalogram analysis, discerns whether or not a sequence of behavioral indices forms an ordinal scale. The method determines whether subjects, in response to a series of items ranked by difficulty, succeed to a certain point and fail all subsequent items. When applied to a series of responses for a group of subjects, the procedure yields an index of consistency *(I),* where any *I* value falling within the range 0.50 to 1.00 is considered to form an ordinal scale. The closer the *I* value is to 1.00, the more invariant is the ordinal sequence.

Uzgiris (1976a) reviewed and analyzed the available data pertaining to the patterns of sequential development among nonhandicapped infants. In all but a very few instances, she found that most investigators have reported *I* values well above the 0.50 minimum necessary for considering a series of items to be invariant. Uzgiris concluded that the available data strongly support Piaget's (1960) contention concerning the sequential and hierarchical acquisition of sensorimotor intelligence.

Only two studies (Kopp, Sigman, & Parmelee, 1973; Miller, Cohen, & Hill, 1970) have reported *I* values below 0.50. However, Kopp et al. attempted to scale intermediate stage placement items, and because of this the results do not necessarily invalidate Piaget's (1960) stage hierarchy criterion. Piaget proposed an invariant order of achievement only for stages and not for substages. Miller et al.'s results have been attributed to a methodological problem (see Uzgiris, 1976a). When corrected, the *I* value in the Miller et al. study exceeded the 0.50 minimum. Overall, the available evidence from studies with nonhandicapped infants provides sufficient support for the contention made by Piaget concerning the ordinal nature of the stage sequence of the sensorimotor period.

The use of Piagetian-based infant scales to assess the sensorimotor performance of handicapped children requires that these individuals manifest behaviors in the same stage progression as has been found with nonhandicapped infants. A review of the available data by Dunst (1978b) revealed that children with diverse handicapping conditions do in fact acquire behaviors in the stage sequence posited by Piaget. The studies reviewed included profoundly and severely retarded persons (Kahn, 1976; Rogers, 1977; Silverstein, Brownlee, Hubbell, & McLean, 1975; Woodward, 1959), mildly and moderately retarded infants (Spritzer, 1973), cerebral palsied children (Tessier, 1969/1970), and thalidomide-afflicted children (Decarie, 1969).

Kahn (1976) reported I values ranging from 0.81 to 1.00 in his study of 63 retarded children using the Uzgiris and Hunt scales as the criterion measure of sensorimotor development. Rogers (1977), examining the characteristics of sensorimotor development among institutionalized retarded children, reported I values of 0.77, 0.57, and 0.75, respectively, for object permanence, causality, and imitation. Silverstein et al. (1975) reported similar I values (0.58 and 0.70) for two object permanence scales (Escalona & Corman, 1966; Uzgiris & Hunt, 1975) in their study of institutionalized severely and profoundly retarded children.

The only branch of development for which ordinality has not been found in studies of retarded children is spatial relationships (Rogers, 1977; Silverstein et al., 1975). However, in both of these investigations, intermediate stage level scaling was attempted. As noted above, not finding ordinality when this is done does not necessarily invalidate Piaget's proposed invariant stage sequence of the sensorimotor period. When Rogers scaled stages rather than intermediate stage level tasks, the I value for spatial relationships increased from 0.33 to 0.79, a value well above the minimum necessary for considering a developmental sequence invariant.

Although the appropriateness of Piagetian-based infant scales has not been specifically examined with sensory-impaired children, the data that are available indicate that the patterns of sensorimotor development among these individuals are similar to those of nonhandicapped infants. Best and Roberts (1976) found that, except for vocal imitation, deaf children did not differ in their level of sensorimotor development (as measured by the Uzgiris and Hunt scales) when compared to nonimpaired children. In extensive descriptive studies by Fraiberg (1968, 1975), blind infants manifested sequential patterns of development very similar to those of sighted children in the acquisition of object and person permanence. That is, blind infants were found to develop the concepts of object and person permanence in a stage level progression analogous to that found for nonimpaired infants. They simply acquired the concepts at a much slower rate.

As a whole, the data that are available concerning the sequential patterns of development among handicapped children strongly support the contention that these individuals acquire sensorimotor skills in the same stage level progression as that originally posited by Piaget (1936, 1937, 1945). However, before Piagetian-based scales can be used with handicapped individuals, one further requirement must be met: the use of such scales must be reliable. Reported interobserver reliability has been quite high (Kahn, 1976; Robinson, Chatelanat, Spritzer, Robertson, & Bricker, 1973; Rogers, 1977; Silverstein et al., 1975). The percentage of agreement between independent observers has generally been in the 0.85 to 0.99 range. Both Kahn (1976) and Robinson et al. (1973) have reported high test-retest reliability in the studies of sensorimotor development they conducted. Using the seven Uzgiris and Hunt scales as criterion measures, Kahn reported stability coefficients for the individual scales that ranged from 0.88 to 0.96, values exceeding those reported by Uzgiris and Hunt (1975) for nonretarded infants. Robinson et al. reported similar coefficients in their study.

The reliability data, in conjunction with the ordinality data reviewed briefly above, provide sufficient support to indicate that Piagetian-based infant scales are appropriate for use with handicapped populations. The remainder of this manual describes one particular approach to the assessment of the sensorimotor performance of retarded and handicapped persons.

THE CLINICAL-EDUCATIONAL PROCESS

The clinical-educational procedure described in this manual is designed to yield data concerning three aspects of a child's sensorimotor development: 1) quantitative characteristics, 2) qualitative characteristics, and 3) information relevant for determining psycho-educational needs.

Quantitative Characteristics

Data used to describe a child's sensorimotor characteristics in quantitative terms consist of EDA placements assigned to each of the sensorimotor landmarks comprising the content of the Uzgiris and Hunt scales. Four types of quantitative information can be derived using these scores. First, a child's performance in each of the seven branches of development can be described in terms of the EDA itself. For example, if the child's highest item passed on the object permanence scale is an 11-month item, it can be said that the child is functioning at *approximately* an 11-month level in that branch of development. Second, a child's average EDA can be determined as a measure of the child's overall quantitative performance. Third, deviation scores (EDAs minus the child's chronological age) can be determined as specific measures of the extent to which a child is retarded or advanced in development for each sensorimotor branch. Fourth, the child's overall degree of developmental delay can be determined by means of an *average deviation* score. The actual procedures used to obtain these scores are described in subsequent sections of this manual. Data to support the validity of these quantitative procedures are presented in Appendix D.

The quantitative procedures described in this manual are not unlike those used in scoring traditional infant tests and other psychometric instruments. These scores provide one basis for determining a child's relative developmental standing using his or her own chronological age as a reference point for determining delays and/or deviations in performance. *This is the only purpose they can serve.* As Lezak (1976) has pointed out, a test score "...only represents one narrowly defined aspect of a set of behavior samples (that) is two or more steps removed from the original behavior" (p. 118). In other words, quantitative scores, despite their communicative utility, provide little or no useful information concerning either a child's actual pattern of performance or the types of experiences best adopted to foster developmental progress. This is one of the major shortcomings of traditional psychometric infant tests. In terms of the overall clinical-educational process, the procedures for determining a child's quantitative performance permit the assessment of a very limited aspect of a child's sensorimotor capabilities and needs. This point is stressed throughout the various sections of this manual.

Qualitative Characteristics

The description of the child's sensorimotor development in qualitative terms represents the most important step in the overall clinical-educational process. The qualitative information obtained is used to determine: 1) the levels of development achieved in each of the seven branches of sensorimotor performance, 2) the child's overall pattern of sensorimotor development, 3) whether this pattern of development is typical or atypical, 4) the extent to which deviations in development are or are not present, and 5) the exact nature of deviations in development, if any.

Three types of data are used to determine the qualitative characteristics of a child's patterns of sensorimotor development. First and most important, the child's development is described in terms of the highest behavior achieved in each of the seven branches of development assessed by the Uzgiris and Hunt scales. This provides concrete and specific data concerning the child's level of performance in each of the seven branches of development. That is, knowledge of the highest landmark achieved provides information concerning the particular point along a developmental continuum at which a child is functioning.

Second, the Piagetian stages corresponding to each of the highest critical behaviors achieved is determined. Inasmuch as stages are intended to index the qualitative changes in the genesis of particular concepts or constructs (e.g., means-ends abilities) (Flavell, 1963), knowledge of the child's developmental standing according to stage placements provides a measure of the types of cognitive operations that the child is capable of performing. For example, if the child is found to be functioning primarily in Stage III of the sensorimotor period (see Table 1), we would know that he or she is able to operate with an understanding that actions directed toward objects (e.g., batting at a mobile) or toward persons (e.g., smiling and vocalizing) have the effect of maintaining the reinforcing consequences (e.g., auditory feedback and an adult producing an interesting facial gesture, respectively) that the behaviors were intended to elicit.

Third, as a measure of the child's variability in performance, a profile of abilities is constructed to graphically portray the child's overall pattern of sensorimotor development. A profile not only depicts the child's major strengths and weaknesses, but it also permits one to pinpoint particular deviations in development if they are present.

The actual procedures involved in determining the qualitative characteristics of a child's sensorimotor development are illustrated in the final section of the manual.

Determining Psychoeducational Needs

The final phase of the clinical-educational process consists of identifying the particular types of experiences best adopted to foster development specific to a child's individual psychoeducational needs. The results of administration of the Uzgiris and Hunt scales are particularly useful in this regard, especially the information obtained concerning the qualitative characteristics of a child's sensorimotor performance.

Three types of psychoeducational intervention activities can be developed based on the results of an assessment of a child's sensorimotor capabilities. First, activities can be developed to facilitate cognitive growth in terms of movement from a lower to a higher level of functioning within particular domains. Second, activities can be developed in which existing sensorimotor abilities are used as a basis for facilitating acquisition of targeted behaviors (e.g., using gestural imitation abilities to foster vocal imitation skills). Third, activities can be developed in which the goal is to integrate and synthesize existing sensorimotor skills to ensure that the infant learns the interrelatedness and functional use of his or her cognitive abilities. All three types of sensorimotor activities are developed within the context of *intervention packages*. An intervention package is a set or series of activities designed to facilitate both the acquisition and synthesis of sensorimotor skills in a manner that optimizes the efficacy of the intervention procedures. Guidelines and a model for utilizing the Uzgiris and Hunt scales to accomplish this goal are described in the final section of the manual.

The use of the Uzgiris and Hunt scales for the purposes described in this manual deviates considerably from the purposes for which the scales were originally intended to be used (see Uzgiris & Hunt, 1975, pp. 17–19). This is true concerning the approach to assessment presented, and is particularly true with regard to the procedures for quantifying sensorimotor performance. For example, Hunt (1972, 1977a) has been extremely adamant concerning the value of numerical scores for describing sensorimotor performance. Readers interested in exploring both alternative uses of the Uzgiris and Hunt scales and arguments regarding the value of quantifying sensorimotor performance are referred to Uzgiris and Hunt's own works (Hunt, 1976, 1977a, 1977b, 1979, in press; Hunt, Mohandessi, Ghodssi, & Akiyama, 1976; Hunt, Paraskevopoulos, Schickedanz, & Uzgiris, 1976; Paraskevopoulos & Hunt, 1971; Uzgiris, 1973, 1976a, 1976b, 1977a, 1977b).

THE NEED FOR CLINICAL RECORD FORMS

In their monograph, Uzgiris and Hunt (1975) provide two kinds of record forms for use in administering their scales. Neither, however, lends itself readily to the clinical-educational use of the scales. Therefore, record forms designed to facilitate the clinical-educational process described above were specifically developed for this manual. These forms are described in more detail in subsequent sections, and are included in Appendix A.

This manual is not intended to be a substitute for Uzgiris and Hunt's monograph (1975) describing their scales, but is rather designed to augment their book for the purposes described above. Therefore, a thorough knowledge of the Uzgiris and Hunt monograph is considered the major prerequisite for use of this manual. In addition to this prerequisite, prospective users should have a working knowledge of Piagetian theory (see e.g., Flavell, 1963; Hunt, 1961; Piaget, 1936, 1937, 1945; Pinard & Laurendeau, 1969), and experience in testing and working with young children. Prospective examiners should also be trained under the supervision of an examiner possessing extensive knowledge and expertise in use of the scales. Other specific procedures usually suggested for training examiners who are to test infants should also be adhered to (see, for example, Bayley, 1969).

The remainder of this manual is divided into three sections: 1) a general description of the record forms, 2) directions for administration and scoring of the scales, and 3) the procedures for recording the assessment results, constructing a profile of abilities, and interpreting and utilizing the findings.

Four appendices are included. Appendix A contains the summary record form, the profile of abilities form, and the seven individual scale record forms. All of these forms are used for the clinical administration of the scales. Appendix B includes the description and procedures for administering the 53 experimental (E) assessment items designed to supplement the 73 scale steps on the Uzgiris and Hunt instrument. Appendix C lists the suggested test materials and equipment that may be used in administration of the scales. Appendix D provides data to support the validity of the quantitative scoring procedures developed for this manual.

GENERAL DESCRIPTION OF THE RECORD FORMS

Each individual scale record form includes eight sections: 1) scale steps, 2) estimated developmental age (EDA) placements, 3) Piagetian stage placements of the scale landmarks, 4) eliciting contexts, 5) critical action codes that identify the assessment items in the Uzgiris and Hunt monograph, 6) the critical behaviors that constitute the sequential developmental landmarks, 7) space for scoring the child's responses, and 8) space for recording observations and responses of particular interest to the examiner. The record forms, along with a summary form and a profile of abilities form, can be found in Appendix A.

The organization of the different sections is designed to aid in the administration, scoring, and interpretation of the scales. The first three sections (scale steps, EDA placements, and Piagetian stages) are intended to provide the examiner with information that is useful for establishing an individual's current developmental status and for interpretation of the results. None of these sections is ordinarily of utility in administration of the scales.

The next three sections (eliciting contexts, critical action codes, and critical behaviors) provide the examiner with the necessary information needed to administer the scales. The eliciting contexts specify the behavioral categories or classes of responses that are to be assessed or observed, whereas the critical behaviors define the ac-

tions that represent the sequential developmental landmarks on each of the scales.

The scoring and observation sections are designed to aid in recording particular behaviors that are elicited, and to ensure that the recording process is proper and systematic. Each of the eight record form sections is discussed in more detail in the remainder of this section.

SCALE STEPS

In constructing ordinal scales of infant psychological development, Uzgiris and Hunt (1975) placed minimal emphasis on replicating Piaget's (1936, 1937, 1945) own observations of sensorimotor development. Instead, they concerned themselves with identifying a greater number of intermediate steps or landmarks that represent successive, hierarchical levels of cognitive performance. The sequence of scale steps identified varied from 7 to 14 for the different branches of development. The object permanence scale includes 14 steps; the means-ends abilities scale has 13 steps; both vocal and gestural imitation have 9 steps; operational causality has 7 steps; the construction of object relations in space scale includes 11 steps; and the schemes for relating to objects scale has 10 steps.

The scale steps for each branch of development are identified on the record forms by arabic numbers. They are, of course, sequentially ordered from the lowest to the highest steps. Four of the scales (vocal imitation, gestural imitation, causality, and spatial relationships) include scale steps with lower-case letters. This indicates that similar responses to the same or different eliciting situations *score at the same developmental level.* For example, scale step number 3 in the causality branch indexes the ability to "use procedures as causal actions to reinstate an interesting spectacle." To test whether or not the child manifests this ability four different assessment situations may be used to elicit this critical behavior: response to an interesting spectacle, response in a familiar game situation, response to a spectacle created by an agent, or response to a spectacle created by an agent acting on an object. A procedure that was elicited in response to any of the situations would represent a scale step 3 behavior, regardless of the particular spectacle or game that elicited the "use of a procedure."

The same system is utilized in scoring several of the landmarks on the vocal and gestural imitation scales. For example, consider scale step number 4 in the gestural imitation branch. The eliciting situations are the modeling of complex gestures composed of familiar schemes and the modeling of unfamiliar, *visible* gestures. If a child imitated either of the two types of behaviors by gradual approximation, the response would represent a scale step 4 behavior.

The one exception to this scoring system occurs on the spatial relationships scale. The eliciting situations for scale step 11 are quite dissimilar, but nevertheless either critical behavior (makes detours or indicates the absence of familiar persons) scores at the same developmental level.

In addition to the 73 developmental scale steps included on the Uzgiris and Hunt scales, 53 experimental (E) items have been added. These items are identified by the upper-case letter E and subscripted numerals. The numeric subscripts are for identification purposes only, and are *not necessarily intended* to represent intervening ordinal scale steps. Their placement is approximately where the critical behaviors would be expected to be manifested. The experimental items have been successively numbered from scale I (object permanence) through scale VI (schemes for relating to objects). The rationale for inclusion of these items is described in the "Critical Behaviors" section below.

ESTIMATED DEVELOPMENTAL AGE PLACEMENTS

Uzgiris and Hunt (1975) seriously question whether standardization of their scales would serve any particularly useful purpose. This doubt stems from a conviction that infant psychological development is affected by experiences encountered by the infant during interaction with his or her caregivers, and the particular environ-

mental circumstances under which the child is reared. Much of the research conducted using the Uzgiris and Hunt scales has supported this contention (e.g., Hunt, 1977a, 1977b; Hunt et al., 1975, 1976; Paraskevopoulos & Hunt, 1972). The mean ages at which groups of infants have achieved the landmarks indexed by certain of the scales have in fact been found to vary substantially as a function of environmental circumstances encountered. Hunt (1977a, 1977b) regards these differences as phenotypic modifications or a "range of reactions" resulting from variations in environmental experiences afforded the infants. Therefore, the value of age norms for the scale steps would be somewhat misleading inasmuch as the age of acquisition of the landmarks reflects the types of experiences that the infants have encountered. Nevertheless, in the clinical use of the scales, it is necessary to have some basis from which to decide the extent to which an individual is advanced or retarded in each of the branches of development. Inasmuch as age continues to be the principle variable used to make such judgments, it was considered essential that at least estimated developmental age (EDA) placements be assigned to each of the scale steps.

Nine major sources were used in determining EDA placements for the scale landmarks (Bayley, 1969; Cattell, 1940; Griffiths, 1954; Kopp et al., 1974; Uzgiris, 1967, 1972, 1973; Uzgiris & Hunt, 1975; White, 1971). In assigning age placements to the scale steps, extreme care was taken to ensure that the data used were not gathered in studies of infants who were reared under either extremely advantageous or extremely detrimental circumstances. Assigning age placements to the landmarks on the object permanence, means-ends, space, and scheme scales was possible with little difficulty, but determining age placements for the vocal imitation, gestural imitation, and causality scales was somewhat more difficult, because very little work has been done concerning development in these particular branches. Caution is especially warranted concerning the age placements of the first four scale steps on the vocal imitation scale. Very little research has been conducted in this area of development, and the available data are conflicting with regard to the ages at which infants manifest the critical behaviors indexed. Whenever a number of successive developmental landmarks have the same EDA placement, it is presumed that the scale steps are ordinarily manifested within a single one-month period of time.

Age placements are intended to have *no normative value,* but nonetheless may be considered estimates of the "modal" age at which children ordinarily attain the scale landmarks. The validity of the EDAs was examined in a study of 36 handicapped and at-risk infants and toddlers administered both the Uzgiris and Hunt (1975) scales and the Griffiths (1954) Mental Development Scales (see Appendix D). The EDAs assigned to the developmental landmarks on the Uzgiris and Hunt scales were found to correlate substantially and significantly with actual psychometric developmental performance. The average of the seven separate EDAs, intended as an estimate of a child's mental age, correlated 0.97 ($P < 0.01$) with actual mental age. Deviation scores (EDAs minus the child's chronological age), intended to measure the degree of developmental delay in each of the separate branches of development, correlated significantly with developmental quotient (DQ) scores on each of the five subscales on the Griffiths test. The average of the seven separate deviation scores, intended as an overall measure of developmental delay, correlated -0.63 ($P < 0.01$) with actual general intelligence quotient (GQ) scores. EDAs, and scores derived from them, therefore seem to have excellent concurrent validity in terms of predicting actual psychometric test performance. (See Appendix D for a detailed description of the concurrent validity study of the EDA scores.)

The EDA placements are provided only to aid the clinician in determining an individual's relative *current* developmental status in each of the seven branches of sensorimotor performance. However, it must be stressed that sensorimotor performance at one level has been found to have little relationship to subsequent levels of development (King & Seegmiller, 1973; Lewis & McGurk, 1972; Uzgiris, 1973), and consequently EDAs have no predictive value. In addition, it must be remembered that EDAs do not contribute to an understanding of a child's actual qualitative pattern of sensorimotor development. Moreover, EDAs are intended to assess a very limited aspect of a child's overall sensorimotor capabilities. Consequently, the limitations of the usefulness of the EDAs must be constantly recognized. As is always the case, "good" clinical judgment should be made in using the EDA placements provided. If they are used to estimate a child's current developmental status, their use must be qualified in terms of both their minimal utility and lack of predictive value.

DEVELOPMENTAL STAGE PLACEMENTS

As already noted, the Uzgiris and Hunt (1975) scales are based, in part, on Piaget's theory of sensorimotor development. Piaget (1936) describes the genesis of infant cognition as occurring through a six-stage process beginning at birth and culminating in the ability to use symbolic–representationally indicative behaviors at around 2 years of age. Each stage in this sequence is defined by behavioral response classes that exemplify distinct levels of cognitive performance (see Table 1 above).

Much of the work on sensorimotor development continues to be presented within this six-stage conceptualization (e.g., Bower, 1974; Corman & Escalona, 1969; Kopp et al., 1974; see, however, Uzgiris, 1976a, 1977b, for arguments against the theoretical utility of stage delineations). Stage placements are useful for several purposes. First, knowledge of the stage placements of the critical behaviors on a particular scale provides a basis for determining which items measure similar cognitive processes (i.e., the same stage abilities) in the branch. Second, because the items on the different scales within the same stage presumably measure parallel sensorimotor skills, the type(s) of cognitive operations that the child is capable of performing can be determined. Third, since performance in one sensorimotor domain is generally unrelated to performance in the other branches of development (Kopp et al., 1974; Uzgiris, 1973, 1976a), it is possible to assess the extent to which a child's sensorimotor capabilities vary by noting the child's range of stage performance. The particular pattern of variability permits a determination of a child's strengths and weaknesses, and the extent to which he or she is showing typical or atypical patterns of development. The use of stage placements for these purposes is illustrated in the final section of this manual.

Besides their utility for the purposes just described, stage placements, together with EDA placements, allow more meaningful statements to be made concerning the child's current developmental status. When considered in relationship to one another, they increase the validity of the assessment findings and conclusions that are made.

In assigning stage placements to the critical behaviors, Piaget's (1936, 1937, 1945) own classification system constituted the principle source of reference. When there was a question concerning a particular critical action, the stage placements of Casati and Lezine (1968) or Escalona and Corman (1966) were used.

ELICITING CONTEXTS

Uzgiris and Hunt (1975, pp. 145-146) provide specific instructions for arranging the eliciting situations to assess the critical behaviors for the various steps on each of the scales. The directions specify: 1) the position of the infant and the nature of the physical environment around the child, 2) the object or objects suggested for use in the situation, 3) the instructions for actions to be carried out by the examiner, 4) the suggested number of times the situation is to be repeated, and 5) the various actions an infant may be expected to show in the situations. It is presumed that the clinician or other individual using the record forms in this manual is intimately familiar with these instructions.

The eliciting context section of the record forms included in this manual provides highly specific identifying information that is intended to *cue* the examiner as to which situation is to be contrived to elicit the critical behaviors indexed, or to specify the type of behavior that is actually to be elicited. Which of these two situations is provided depends on the scale items themselves.

To illustrate the utility of the eliciting context section, consider the five consecutive items on the object permanence scale titled "Visible Displacements." This eliciting code should cue the examiner that a series of items are to be presented where the child is going to be required to secure an object *seen* hidden under one or more screens. A glance at the critical behavior section then specifies the exact visible displacement behavior(s) to be assessed.

With a little experience, the examiner should find the information provided in the eliciting context section useful for enhancing the ease of presentation of the assessment items.

CRITICAL ACTION CODES

Each of the seven scales on the Uzgiris and Hunt assessment instrument includes from 4 to 15 eliciting situations that are used to determine whether the child possesses a range of different cognitively indicative behaviors. Each eliciting situation includes a number of possible infant actions that might be observed in response to a particular testing procedure (i.e., eliciting situation). Uzgiris and Hunt (1975) have designated one or more of these possible infant actions as "critical" actions.

Critical actions are those behaviors that "...imply that an infant has attained a particular level of functioning in a given branch of development" (Uzgiris & Hunt, 1975, p. 49). The critical actions (i.e., the behaviors that are manifested) determine the child's performance levels in each of the branches of development. The critical action code sections of the record forms identify the relevant eliciting situation and critical infant action for each of the successive developmental landmarks. The arabic numbers identify the *eliciting situation* used to assess the critical behaviors, and the lower case letters identify the *critical actions* that correspond to the record form critical behaviors (i.e., the adjacent right-hand section). For example, scale step 5 on the object permanence scale indexes the ability to secure an object hidden under a single screen. The fourth eliciting situation on the Uzgiris and Hunt scales is used to assess whether or not the child manifests this ability. The "d" critical infant action is the behavior that must be observed in order to credit the child with "secures an object hidden under a single screen."

Note that there is no one-to-one correspondence between the eliciting situations and the scale steps. *Eliciting situations are often confused for scale steps.* This is a misinterpretation. The record forms developed for this manual are designed, in part, to alleviate such a misunderstanding.

The critical action code section does not generally enter into the administration of the scales. The information is provided so that the examiner can quickly identify the items in the Uzgiris and Hunt monograph. The critical action codes provide a ready-made index to the more complete descriptions of the eliciting situations by Uzgiris and Hunt, should there be any need to consult them.

CRITICAL BEHAVIORS

Each of the record forms lists in ascending order the critical behaviors (i.e., developmental landmarks) that represent the successive levels of sensorimotor performance for each of the seven branches. The experimental scale items have been inserted in this sequence at the approximate level where the behaviors indexed would be expected to be attained.

The scale step descriptions retain essential information from both the eliciting situations and critical infant actions described by Uzgiris and Hunt (1975) so as to render the critical behaviors on the record forms substantially self-explanatory for persons familiar with Uzgiris and Hunt's monograph. When considered in conjunction with the eliciting contexts, the examiner is provided with sufficient information to administer the scale item and to record whether or not the critical behavior is elicited. For example, on the means-ends scale, the eliciting context for scale step number 6 indicates that a "support" item is to be administered. The critical behavior section then specifies the behavior to be observed ("pulls support to obtain an object placed on it").

Extensive experience using the Uzgiris and Hunt scales, particularly with handicapped and retarded children, has revealed that, despite their general utility, the scales have a number of shortcomings when used for clinical and educational purposes. One problem is that, at various developmental stages, too few items are provided to establish an accurate picture of an individual's current performance status. In addition, presumably because handicapped and retarded infants take longer to progress through the sensorimotor period, many more intermediate steps or levels can often be identified in particular developmental areas. Thus, it was deemed essential that several additional measures be utilized to fill in the apparent gaps. The inclusion of the experimental (E) items is intended to augment the already existing battery of 73 scale steps on the Uzgiris and Hunt assessment instrument for this purpose.

The description of the procedures for administering and scoring the experimental items is presented in Appendix B. A number of the developmental landmarks were implicated by Uzgiris and Hunt (1975) as possible intermediate scale steps; other critical behaviors have been adapted from a number of other sources, but primarily from the Piagetian-based scales constructed by Casati and Lezine (1968) and Escalona and Corman (1966). The examiner should find many of the experimental items helpful as alternative procedures for assessing the same stage cognitive abilities that the Uzgiris and Hunt items assess. It is well to keep in mind, however, that the manifestation of an experimental item critical behavior before or after the adjacent Uzgiris and Hunt scale steps does not invalidate the presumed ordinality of the developmental sequence posited by Uzgiris and Hunt (1975). Rather, it indicates that the experimental item represents a developmental ability at a level other than where placed on the record form. The scalability of the E items requires further study. Until such investigations are conducted, the examiner must remain cognizant of the *approximate* placement of the E items in the Uzgiris and Hunt sequences.

SCORING SYSTEM

The scoring system that is recommended in using the record forms includes seven scoring/recording categories:

(+)   Critical behavior is elicited in response to the particular assessment item designed to measure whether the child manifests the scale landmark. A response is also scored (+) if it is observed during the course of the examination and the context of its occurrence meets the requirements of the eliciting situation designed to assess the behavior.

(✔)   Critical behavior is manifested following *demonstration* of the behavior by the examiner. The Uzgiris and Hunt (1975) monograph should be consulted when actually scoring the child's responses to determine if a behavior elicited following a demonstration (✔) may be scored as a (+).

(±)   Indicates that the critical behavior is emerging and that the child's response to the eliciting situation includes components of the critical behavior. *The emerging response observed should be noted in the observation section.*

(−)   Critical behavior is not manifested in response to the appropriate eliciting situation and/or is not observed during the examination period. The child's actual response should be noted in the observation section. It is especially important to note whether a child made *no response* or a response that reflected minimal appreciation for the needed requirements to complete the task. The latter information is especially useful for identifying potential learning difficulties.

(O) Eliciting situation designed to assess the child's ability to perform the critical behavior is omitted (i.e., not presented).

(R) Critical behavior is neither elicited nor observed. However, it is reported by the parent or parent surrogate that the child performs the behavior at home or in another context. The particular situation and/or context in which the behavior is reported to be manifested should be noted in the observation section on the record form.

(M) Indicates a mistrial. An eliciting situation is presented but, before completing the presentation, the child is distracted and/or turns away from the examiner, or the item was not presented correctly. Mistrials are not counted as presentations.

Only (+) and (✓) scores are used in assessing whether or not the child has attained a given level of performance.

The record forms provide space for up to five presentations of any one eliciting situation, although it is usually not necessary to present that many assessment items to determine whether or not an individual manifests the critical behavior under observation. Specific instructions for scoring the individual scale items are presented in Section 3 of the manual.

OBSERVATION SECTION

The observation section of the record forms is provided for the examiner to note behaviors and/or responses that are of particular interest. The examiner may, for example, wish to make notes concerning the child's emotional state changes (e.g., smiling, laughing, crying, distressfulness) in response to particular scale items. These data would be especially useful if interventions were to be suggested. Knowing what the child particularly liked or disliked, what elicited positive and negative responses, and so forth would enhance the examiner's ability to make appropriate recommendations.

Three of the scales (vocal imitation, gestural imitation, and operational causality) include convenient notation headings in the observation section. These are designed to aid the examiner in recording the particular behavior(s) presented as part of the eliciting situation and for noting the response(s) made by the child. The appearance of notation headings in the observation section of the record forms indicates that any number of behaviors can be expected to be manifested in responses to a *single* eliciting situation. The responses included as part of the notation heading are the particular behavioral categories that score at different developmental levels on the scale. For example, the notation heading for scale step 2a on the vocal imitation scale includes: sound presented, positive response (elicited), vocalizes (in response to), and imitates. If, say, the sound "ah-goo" were presented, and the child responded by producing the sound "ah-ee," the examiner would simply record under the notation heading subsection of "vocalizes" the sound elicited. The child would then be given credit for achieving scale step number 3 ("vocalizes in response to cooing sounds").

When a notation heading is to be used for a series of scale steps, the heading appears at the first developmental level in the sequence. On both the vocal and gestural imitation scales, *all* the critical behaviors indexed can be scored from the information recorded in the notational headings. Therefore, in using the record forms, it is only necessary to note which behaviors are presented (i.e., the eliciting situations), and record the responses observed in the notation headings. From this information, the entire scale can be scored after completing the administration of the eliciting situations.

Beginning with scale step number 3 on the operational causality scale, notation headings are provided that include the game, action, or spectacle presented and the "procedure" or "other causal action" that the child used to have the examiner repeat the interesting event. If the examiner carefully records the exact behavior(s) used by the child as causal actions, all subsequent scale steps, except the E items, can be scored from the information recorded in the notation headings.

DIRECTIONS FOR ADMINISTRATION AND SCORING

In administering the scales, both the general instructions and the specific directions that Uzgiris and Hunt (1975, pp. 143–204) provide in their monograph should be followed. It is essential that the examiner be intimately familiar with the directions and procedures provided for arranging the eliciting situations. This information is provided in Chapters 11 through 16 of Uzgiris and Hunt's (1975) book describing the scales. In addition to these instructions, other directions that should be followed when administering the scales are presented in this section. These supplemental instructions pertain specifically to the clinical use of the scales, and are designed to aid the examiner in establishing accurate developmental performance levels in each of the sensorimotor domains assessed.

GENERAL CONSIDERATIONS

As is the case with all infant testing procedures, certain minimal conditions should be met to ensure that optimal performance from the infant is obtained. Some of the more basic considerations are briefly mentioned here.

Rapport between Examiner and Child

Any attempt to determine an infant's sensorimotor capabilities necessitates that an excellent rapport be established between the examiner and child. On the arrival of the parent and child at the examination room, or the examiner's arrival at the child's home if the assessment is to be conducted there, the child should be permitted to stay near the parent until he or she shows some interest in the examiner or the test materials. During this "warm-up" period, the examiner should direct his or her first remarks to the parent—explaining the purpose of the assessment, describing briefly the types of behaviors that will be examined, recording background information, and so on. Once these introductory matters have been concluded, the examiner should call the child's attention to the test materials, and attempt to elicit some indication that he or she wishes to play with them.

The flexibility of administering ordinal scales, particularly with respect to the scheme scale, permits the child to play with the test materials in any way he or she desires. Allowing the child to do so is often an excellent means for establishing examiner-child rapport. When specific assessment items are presented, they should be administered in a playful manner and not be viewed as demand situations. The more easygoing the assessment is, the more likely optimal performance will be obtained.

Environmental Considerations

The assessment can be conducted either in a clinic or classroom setting or in the child's home. Whichever location is used, it should be pleasant but devoid of extraneous toys, materials, and noises (e.g., a radio) that might distract the child.

For assessments conducted in a clinic or classroom setting, the minimal equipment required includes an infant seat, a high chair, and both adult-size and child-size tables and chairs. The room itself should be comfortable, well-lighted, and adequately ventilated. The lighting, however, should not produce unnecessary glare from the table surfaces or toys. Young infants are especially distracted by fluorescent lights, which often precludes an accurate assessment of the child's performance levels. Care should be taken to eliminate this distraction if present.

When testing handicapped and retarded children, it is extremely important that the child's position be such that any potential intervening problems (e.g., lack of head control) be minimized as variables that might prevent obtaining optimal performance.

Order of Presentation of the Scales

There is no specified order of presentation of the scales. On the contrary, it is better to move from one scale to another to maintain the interest of the child. However, as already noted, it is often best to begin with the schemes for relating to objects scale, since many of the items can be scored from the spontaneous play behavior of the child.

For beginning examiners who often feel the need to administer a single scale at a time, it is suggested that they administer three to four successive items on one scale and then switch to another, returning to each scale at a later time to complete the assessment.

Throughout the assessment, the examiner should be aware of the child's spontaneous imitation of both vocal and gestural behaviors, and should record the responses in the appropriate spaces provided in the notation headings in the observation section of the record forms.

Although it is possible for an experienced examiner to administer all the scales in a single test session, it is generally better to extend the assessment over 2 or 3 days if possible to ensure that optimal performance is obtained.

Where to Begin the Assessment

It is not necessary, nor is it feasible, to administer the entire battery of assessment items. In fact, the nature of several of the scales often makes it impossible to elicit lower-level behaviors once more mature behaviors have been acquired. For example, if the child has learned to give a toy to an adult as a causal action to have the adult activate it, any attempt to elicit "procedures" as causal actions would be unlikely to succeed.

Because lower-level behaviors are generally replaced by higher-level action patterns (particularly on the vocal imitation, gestural imitation, causality, and scheme scales), the place to begin the assessment cannot be conveniently stated. However, from causal observations of the child during the "warm-up" period and by questioning the parent, the stage of development at which items should first be administered can generally be ascertained. It is "good" clinical practice to begin the assessment with items that are developmentally two or three steps below the level at which the child is considered to be functioning. This will ensure initial success on the child's part, and consequently will help to maintain the child's interest throughout the assessment.

INSTRUCTIONS PERTAINING TO THE INDIVIDUAL SCALES

For each individual scale, three considerations pertaining to clinical administration are discussed: suggested guidelines for eliciting optimal performance, the range of items to be administered, and the criteria for scoring and determining an individual's performance level. These procedures and instructions are designed to supplement those described by Uzgiris and Hunt (1975) in their monograph. Where differing procedures and scoring instructions are discussed, those of this manual take precedence in the clinical and educational use of the scales.

Object Permanence

In administering the visual tracking items, care should be taken to ensure that the visual field immediately to the front and sides of the child is void of extraneous stimuli that might interfere with accurate assessment of visual following behaviors. This is particularly important for items E_2, 4, and E_3, where, when the object moves out of the visual field, the child is expected to search for the object at the point of disappearance, or to reverse searching in anticipation of the object's reappearance from the child's other side.

When administering the various hiding tasks on the object permanence scale, it is important to avoid allowing the child to get into a "set" of just pulling off the screens, expecting by trial and error to sooner or later secure the displaced object. If it appears that the child has begun doing so, administration of the scale items should be discontinued. The examiner should go on to another scale and then return later to complete the object permanence assessment.

Often, it is possible to determine if the child is just pulling off screens by covering nothing and observing the child's response. If the child pulls the cloth, apparently looking for an object, he or she probably got into the set of "pull cloth-obtain object."

Items to be Administered   Present at least three to four items below the child's apparent ceiling level, and obtain failures on at least two successive items above ceiling performance.

A maximum of three to five eliciting situations should be presented for each scale step. In other words, the test procedure used to measure whether or not a child manifests a given behavior should not be presented more than 5 times.

Scoring   The child's ceiling performance is the level at which three critical behaviors elicited in succession are followed by the failure to elicit three successes at the two subsequent levels.

Means-Ends Abilities

This scale is particularly easy to administer, and generally the items are self-explanatory. However, there is often some problem with administering item 8 ("does not pull support with object held above it"). Many children pull the support, not because they do not understand that the object is not on it, but because they seem to want to get the obstacle out of the way (E_{10}) in order to make the desired object more accessible. Item E_{11} was added to the means-ends scale to provide an alternative procedure for determining whether the child actually understands the relationship between the support and the object as the task is intended.

In administering items E_{14}, E_{15}, E_{16}, 12, E_{17}, 13, E_{18}, and E_{19}, it is often necessary to "stabilize" the test materials for the child, particularly for a child with a motor handicap, in order to minimize any possible confounding factors. This is an important consideration since the purpose of the assessment items is not to measure motor maturity, but to measure cognitive performance—specifically, problem-solving abilities.

Items to be Administered   Present at least four to five items below the child's apparent ceiling level and obtain failures on three to four successive items above ceiling performance. The greater range of abilities is necessitated by the fact that the developmental distances between many of the items on this scale appear quite small, thus making the possibility of obtaining a false ceiling at least somewhat likely. By sampling the child's performance over a greater range of items, this possibility is diminished considerably.

A maximum of three to four eliciting situations should be presented for each scale step.

Scoring   The child's ceiling performance is the level at which three out of four critical behaviors noted in response to a particular eliciting situation are followed by the failure to elicit three successes at the three subsequent levels.

Vocal Imitation

During the "warm-up" period before beginning the assessment, the examiner should obtain from the parent or parent surrogate a list of vocalizations and/or words that the child has been heard to produce. These should first be recorded in the observation section provided for scale step 1. When attempting to ascertain what vocalizations the child makes, parents often do not perceive certain of the child's sound productions as constituting vocal patterns. For example, parents often do not report that the child uses throaty "gaa" or other cooing sounds, unless asked specifically by the examiner. Therefore, it is a good practice to ask, by way of example, "Does your child make sounds like _____?"

Besides asking the parent what sounds the child makes, any spontaneous vocalizations heard before and during the course of the assessment should also be recorded in the space provided in the observation section for scale step 1.

Once the range of sound patterns produced by the child has been determined, each vocalization should be recorded in the appropriate notation heading section (cooing, babbling, or familiar words) provided on the record forms. The operational distinction between the five categories of vocalizations is as follows.

Cooing sounds: Sounds or sound patterns that include predominantly vowel sounds (e.g., ah, ooo, ah-ei, goo, uh-ah).

Babbling sounds: Sounds or sound patterns that include consonant and vowel sounds (e.g., da-da, ma-ma, ba-ba, ah-da-da, ba-ah-da).

Familiar words: Adult words or approximations of words that are either produced by the child or regularly used by an adult in the presence of the child (e.g., baby, bye-bye, hello, daddy, mommy).

Unfamiliar sound patterns: Sounds or sound patterns that are *neither* produced by the child nor regularly used by an adult in the presence of the child (e.g., ree-ree, zzz, ssss, bbrrr). It is generally best *not* to include babbling-type sounds (e.g., ma-ma, da-da) in this category, even if the child does not use the sound patterns.

Unfamiliar words: Adult words that are known not to be used by the child or not to be used regularly by an adult in the presence of the child (e.g., pretty, uppity, bear, bunny, flower). Words to be used to assess imitation of unfamiliar words should be ones that the child is likely to imitate if capable of doing so.

Items to be Administered Generally, it is best to sample the child's responses to three or four categories of vocalizations. For example, if it is reported and/or observed that the child produces predominantly cooing and babbling sounds, the child's responses to these sounds plus familiar words and unfamiliar sound patterns would be assessed. However, if it is clinically obvious that attempting to elicit imitative responses beyond the cooing and babbling categories is not possible, there is no need to present unfamiliar sound patterns, although familiar words should be presented.

If it is reported and/or observed that the child produces only a very limited range of vocalizations, or none at all, sound patterns that exemplify cooing, babbling, and unfamiliar sound patterns should nonetheless be presented to ascertain the child's responsiveness to these sounds. In many cases, children discriminate between highly familiar and novel sounds or words by responding "positively" to the former, but remaining inattentive to the latter. Eliciting such a discrimination would at least indicate that the child's ability to differentiate between familiar and unfamiliar sounds is present.

In the actual administration of the vocal imitation scale, the examiner need *only* record the child's responses in the appropriate notation heading sections. From these recorded data, all intermediate scale steps can be scored, and the child's performance level determined. Again, it is important to record exactly what responses are made by the child, and not just check off the category under the notation heading. For example, if the babbling sound "da-da" is presented and the child responds by saying "ba-ba," the particular sound elicited should be recorded under the subheading "vocalizes" on the record form.

It has been found that it is often difficult for some examiners to make a distinction among "vocalizes in response to," "vocalizes similar sounds," "imitates," and so forth when attempting to ascertain the level of vocal imitation at which the child is functioning. Table 2 is provided as a guide to the clinician for determining whether the child's responses to certain sounds represents one of the three categories of responses indicated above.

At least four different sounds or words should be presented within each vocalization category. During the course of the assessment, each vocalization may be presented on six to eight occasions. During a single presentation of a given sound pattern (i.e., on a single occasion), it may be repeated up to 5 times. For example, the examiner might present "ba-ba" followed by a pause; then present the sound again, followed by another pause, and so on.

Scoring The child's ceiling performance is the level at which either the same sound pattern (e.g., ba-ba) elicits the same response on three occasions (e.g., imitates), or three different sound patterns (e.g., ba-ba, da-da, ma-ma) elicit the same response (e.g., a positive response) followed by the failure to elicit three successes at the three subsequent levels. The exceptions to this scoring procedure occur for items E_{24}, E_{25}, and 9, where specific numbers of novel words must be imitated to receive credit for the levels of imitation indicated.

Gestural Imitation

All nine levels of gestural imitation posited by Uzgiris and Hunt are scored from the child's responses to four types of modeled gestural actions: familiar simple gestures, familiar complex gestures, *visible* unfamiliar gestures, and *invisible* unfamiliar gestures. The operational distinction between the four categories of gestural behaviors is as follows.

Familiar simple gesture: A simple, repetitious motor movement, usually an up-and-down motion (e.g., patting a table, shaking a rattle) that the child is known to perform often during play with objects.

Complex familiar gesture: A motor movement composed of familiar simple gestures (i.e., ones the child is known to perform) that are combined to form a complex action. The majority of such actions are back-and-forth across the midline behaviors (e.g., hitting two blocks together), but other behaviors that require differentiated motor actions also constitute complex gestures (e.g., sliding beads along a table surface, stirring a spoon in a cup).

Table 2. Scoring standards for the four categories of responses on the vocal imitation scale

Vocal category	Examples of sounds presented	Elicited behaviors according to response category		
		Vocalizes in response to	Vocalizes similar sounds	Imitates
Cooing	ah	ee, goo, ooh	ga, ha, ya, uh	ah, ah-ah
	ah-goo	ooh, ah, ga	ah-ee, ah-ooh, ya-goo	ah-goo, ahgoogoo
	ga	ee, ooh, goo	ah, ya, ha, uh	ga, ga-ga
Babbling	ba-ba	ah-da, da-ga, ah-goo	ma-ma, da-da, bu-bu	ba-ba, ahbababa
	da-da	ah-goo, ooo, ee	ma-ma, ba-ba, de-de	da-da, daahda
	pu-pu	da-da, ooh, ah	pu-oh, pa-pa, duh-duh	pu-pu, poo-poo
Familiar words	mommy	da-da, ba-ee, ah-ma	ma-ma, ma-ee, ma-ah	mommy, ma-me
	baby	ma-ma, ah-oo, ya-ah	ba-ba, ah-be, ba-da	baby, ba-ee
	bye-bye	ee-oo, da-da, ba-ba	bu-bu, bi-ee, ah-bye	bye-bye, bi-bi
Unfamiliar sound patterns	room-room	da-da, ra-ra, ooh-ooh	re-re, oom-oom, soom	room-room, rum-rum
	ssss	sa-sa, ma-ma, ee-ee	ppzz, eezz, suuu	ssss, sszz
	brrr	ba-ba, ra-ra, da-da	beee, rur	brrr, bru, bur
Novel words	beads	ba-ba, eees, da-da	bees, eads, be-tees	beads, be-dees
	pretty	pa-pa, te-te, ee-ee	pu-ee, pre-ie, et-tee	pretty, pur-tee
	nice	ii-ee, na-na, ne-ne	ni-ee, ice	nice, ni-see

Unfamiliar visible gesture: A motor movement that the child can see him/herself perform, but that is novel and thus is not likely to be performed as a regular part of the child's play (e.g., making the fingers "walk," snapping the fingers).

Unfamiliar invisible gesture: A motor movement, usually performed with the hand touching a certain part of the face or head, that the child cannot see him/herself perform without the use of a mirror (e.g., pulling on the earlobe, touching the back of the neck, wrinkling the nose). Eye, tongue, and mouth movements *should not* be used as invisible gestures since they by necessity constitute a major portion of the child's behavioral repertoire and in fact, when imitated, are Stage IV abilities (Piaget, 1945) rather than Stage V actions, which unfamiliar invisible gestures are intended to assess.

Whether a behavior is familiar or unfamiliar can be determined from observations of the child's play with objects and by questioning the parent to ascertain whether or not the child ordinarily performs the behavioral act of interest.

Items to be Administered The child's responses to all four categories of gestures should be sampled, particularly when testing older handicapped or retarded children. Quite often, these children bypass imitating unfamiliar visible gestures but will imitate or attempt to imitate unfamiliar invisible gestures. This appears to be the case because unfamiliar visible gestures generally involve fine motor movements using the fingers and hands, and tend to be actions that are difficult for some children to perform.

At least four different gestural actions should be presented within each imitation category. During the course of the assessment, each gesture may be presented 3 to 4 times. During a single presentation of a particular gesture (i.e., on a single occasion), it may be repeated up to 5 times.

In administering the gestural imitation scale, the examiner need *only* record the child's responses in the appropriate notation heading for the four types of gestural behaviors. All intermediate items can be scored from these data. Information that is as specific as possible regarding the child's responses to the modeled actions should be recorded.

Scoring The child's ceiling performance is the level at which either the same gesture elicits the same response on three occasions, or three different gestures elicit the same response followed by the

Table 3. Examples of actions used to elicit causal behaviors

Familiar games[a]	Spectacles created by an agent without an object	Spectacles created by an agent with an object[b]
Tickling the child's tummy	Snapping the fingers	Producing a whistling sound by blowing into a pop-bead
"Nibbling" on the child's fingers	Pat-a-cake	Opening and closing a Slinky
Playing peek-a-boo	"Beeping" the nose	Activating a "Farmer says" type of toy
Playing "so-big"	Producing a popping sound by opening and closing the mouth	Producing a squeaking sound by patting a squeeze toy
Blowing on the child's forehead	Producing a whistling sound by blowing into the hands	Making a feather float by blowing it

[a]Games are considered familiar if the parent reports that he/she plays the game with the child as an ordinary part of child-parent play interactions; otherwise, such games represent "spectacles created by an agent *without* an object."

[b]"Spectacles created by an agent *with* an object" differ from "response to an interesting spectacle" (scale step 3a) in that the child appreciates *only* his/her role as a causal agent in the latter, whereas in the former, the child appreciates *both* his/her role and the role of the adult as causal agents.

failure to elicit three successes at the three subsequent levels. The exceptions to this scoring procedure occur for items E_{30}, 8, E_{31}, E_{32}, E_{33}, and 9, where specific numbers of novel, invisible gestures must be imitated to receive credit for the levels of imitation indicated.

Operational Causality

Of all the scales, the operational causality sequence is generally the most difficult to administer, particularly when testing handicapped or retarded children. This seems to be the case for two reasons. First, it is often difficult to identify spectacles, games, or actions that are of interest to the child. Second, it is often difficult to be sure that a child is using a particular behavioral response as a causal action to have the examiner reinstate the spectacle presented.

To aid the examiner in identifying spectacles, actions, and games that can be used to assess the child's level of causal understanding, Table 3 presents a list of behaviors that have been used with fairly good success. Three types of eliciting actions are presented (familiar games, spectacles created by the examiner *without* an object, and spectacles created by the examiner *using* an object). The three types of actions correspond, respectively, to eliciting sit-uations 4, 5, and 6 as described by Uzgiris and Hunt (1975, pp. 188-191).

The problem of whether or not a child is in fact using a particular behavior as a causal action is generally encountered with regard to three types of behaviors: use of procedures (scale step 3), touches adult or object (scale step 4), and gives object to the examiner (scale step 5). The following suggestions and guidelines are offered to aid the examiner in determining whether the child's response is a causal action.

Procedure: Procedures are generally idiosyncratic behaviors that the child uses as an attempt to have the examiner maintain or reinstate an interesting action, game, or spectacle. Procedures might include vocalizations, arm waving, leg kicking, generalized excitement, banging on a table surface, or any combination of these.

To be credited with "uses a procedure as a causal action," the behavior(s) used as a procedure must be performed only after the examiner has ceased presenting the spectacle. That is, after the examiner has presented the spectacle a number of times, followed by a pause of about 5 seconds, the child must consistently perform the procedure as an apparent attempt to have the spectacle reinstated. If the behavior(s) are performed during the presentation of the spectacle, or continue after the spectacle is reinstated, credit as a procedure is not given.

Touches adult or object: To receive credit for touches adult or object to have an interesting spectacle reinstated, the touching action must be deliberate and of short duration, followed by the child waiting and watching the examiner to see if he or she will repeat the action. Repetitious banging on the adult or object *does not* constitute a "touch" causal action. However, if the repetitious banging is followed by a pause, the child may be credited with "uses a procedure."

Gives object to adult: Generally, following the activation of a mechanical toy or production of a spectacle created with an object, children capable of understanding the examiner's role as causal agent will hand the object back to the examiner to have the spectacle recreated. However, many children will push the toy toward the adult as an apparent causal action. To receive credit for "gives toy to adult as a causal action," the child must purposefully push the toy directly to the examiner. Random, nondirected pushing of the object does not receive credit as a causal action. The difference is one of degree, but generally if pushing is used as a causal action, the child will wait following the pushing action to see if the examiner will repeat the spectacle.

Items to be Administered If the child manifests the ability to engage in repetitious motor actions with toys (secondary circular reactions—scale step 2), the child's responses to the following eliciting situations should be sampled: response to familiar games, response to actions produced by the examiner *without* a toy, response to actions created by the examiner *with* a toy, and response to the action produced by a mechanical wind-up toy.

At least three different familiar games and spectacles created by the examiner both *without* and *with* an object should be presented. During the course of the assessment, each eliciting action may be presented on three to four occasions. During a single presentation, a particular action may be repeated up to 4 or 5 times.

Scoring The child's ceiling performance is the level at which either the same spectacle, game, or action elicits the same causal behavior on three occasions, or three different spectacles, games, or actions elicit the same causal behavior followed by the failure to elicit three successes at the two subsequent levels.

Spatial Relationships

This scale is particularly easy to administer, and many of the critical behaviors are observed incidently during the course of the assessment. However, the difficulty in administering two items (7 and 8) necessitated the addition of several E items to provide a better basis for accurate assessment of a child's performance abilities in this branch of development.

Scale step 7 is designed to assess a child's appreciation of the three-dimensionality and functional side of objects. Generally, it is easy to elicit "rotation of the child's bottle" to place the nipple end in the feeding position. However, attempting to elicit rotation of a doll or plastic animal to place the face side within view often is quite difficult. Therefore, items E_{39} (rotates mirror to view self) and E_{40} (turns picture or photograph over to view functional side) were added as alternative measures of the scale step 7 behavior.

Scale step 8 measures the child's ability to understand the relationship between objects (blocks and cup), and the child's action in relationship to the blocks and cup (dumping them out). However, because it is easier to remove the blocks one at a time when they are inside the cup, attempting to elicit "turns the container over to remove the objects inside" is often difficult. Item E_{45} (dumps objects out of a narrow-necked container) was added as an alternative measure of the scale step 8 critical behavior. If the child demonstrates the ability to perform E_{45} and E_{41} (places objects into a container), but does not perform both components together, he or she should nonetheless be given credit for achieving scale step 8.

Items to be Administered Present at least five to six items below the child's apparent ceiling level and obtain failures on five to six successive items above ceiling performance. The greater range of abilities is necessitated both by the fact that the largest number of deviations in acquiring the landmarks in the posited ordinal sequence of any scale has been found to occur in spatial relationships (Uzgiris, 1973), and because of the large number of E items that have been included on this scale.

A maximum of three to four eliciting situations should be presented for each scale step.

Scoring　The child's ceiling performance is the level at which three out of four critical behaviors observed in response to a particular eliciting situation are followed by the failure to elicit three successes at the four subsequent levels.

Schemes for Relating to Objects

The eliciting situations for assessing the child's schemes for relating to objects are grouped according to three types of behaviors: 1) infant actions with simple objects, 2) infant actions on several objects available together, and 3) infant actions on objects having social meaning. The critical behaviors comprising the content of this scale are determined in response to the child's spontaneous behaviors applied to objects within these three groupings. It is important, therefore, that a variety of different toys and materials from each group be offered to the child during the course of the assessment in order to be sure that the child's repertoire of scheme actions has been adequately sampled. This is particularly true with regard to scale steps E_{51}, 8, E_{52}, and 9. Appendix C includes a list of objects that have been found to be especially effective for eliciting socially instigated and giving and showing behaviors.

Although Uzgiris and Hunt (1975) do not differentiate between socially instigated actions performed on oneself and those performed on inanimate objects (e.g., a doll), a distinction is made between these behaviors on the record form. A recent study by Lowe (1975) found that these behaviors represented distinct developmental abilities. Therefore, care should be taken to record whether the actions are restricted to behaviors that involve primarily animate objects (the child, parent, examiner, etc.) or are applied to inanimate objects as well. The latter are considered by Piaget (1945) to be Stage V abilities and the precursors of symbolic play, whereas the former are Stage IV manifestations.

Items to be Administered　For each object group eliciting situation on the scale, at least five to eight objects, toys, and/or materials that could potentially elicit the 10 major critical behaviors that Uzgiris and Hunt have identified as the landmarks in this branch of development should be presented during the course of the assessment.

Scoring　The child's ceiling performance is the level at which at least three examples of the same category of behaviors (e.g., visually monitored dropping) are elicited by three *different* toys, objects, and/or materials, followed by the failure to observe three behaviors within the two successive behavioral categories.

RECORDING, PROFILING, AND INTERPRETING THE RESULTS

The recording, profiling, and interpretation process is designed to facilitate accurate summarization and utilization of the results for both clinical and educational purposes. If the examiner has followed the guidelines and recommendations presented in the preceding sections, recording and profiling the child's sensorimotor abilities is rapid. Although interpretation of the results for clinical purposes is straightforward, utilization of the results for making educational recommendations requires a certain amount of experience in using the scales. Guidelines for use of the assessment results for education and intervention purposes are presented in the final part of this section.

RECORDING THE CHILD'S SENSORIMOTOR ABILITIES

The *Summary Record Form* included in Appendix A is used for recording and summarizing the results of the assessment. On the top part of the form, space is provided for recording the child's name, sex, and date of birth, the date the scales were administered, and the examiner's name. The child's chronological age (CA) should be computed using the space provided on the top right-hand section of the Summary Record Form. The child's CA is computed by subtracting the child's date of birth from the date of testing. (For computational

purposes all months are considered to have 30 days.) Once the child's CA in months and days has been calculated, his or her CA should be rounded off (adjusted) to the nearest month or half-month. If this number of days is 10 or less, round off to the next lowest month; if the number of days is 11 to 20 inclusive, round off to a half-month; if the number of days is 21 or greater, round off to the next highest month. For example, CAs of 8 months and 4 days, 15 months and 17 days, and 11 months and 25 days would, respectively, be rounded off to 8, 15.5, and 12 months. The adjusted CA should be recorded in the space provided on the Summary Record Form.

Space is also provided on the top part of the Summary Record Form for the examiner to record comments and remarks. The examiner may, for example, wish to note the place of testing, the test conditions, the reason the scales are being administered, and the examiner's overall judgment of the assessment (e.g., fair, average, or excellent). The examiner may also want to note such things as the child's exceptionality (if any), the child's social and emotional responsiveness to both the examiner and the assessment procedures, and the child's attention span during the assessment. As the experienced clinician knows, this kind of supplemental information can help qualify statements that are made and conclusions that are drawn concerning the child's developmental status.

The middle section of the Summary Record Form is designed to aid the examiner in transferring and summarizing the results from the individual scale record forms. To transfer the assessment information from each of the separate scale record forms, the following procedure is recommended.

1. Beginning with the object permanence scale, record in the space provided the highest critical behavior manifested by the child in this domain.
2. Record in the space provided the scale step corresponding to this critical behavior. (This information is utilized for constructing the child's profile of sensorimotor abilities.)
3. Both the Piagetian stage placement and estimated developmental age (EDA) placement corresponding to the highest critical behavior achieved should then be recorded in the space provided.
4. Subtract from the child's *adjusted* CA the EDA placement corresponding to the highest critical behavior achieved, and enter this score in the space beneath the heading labeled "Deviation Score." Under conditions where the adjusted CA is larger than the EDA placement, the deviation obtained will be a minus (−) score. When the adjusted CA is smaller than the EDA placement, the obtained deviation will be a plus (+) score.
5. Repeat the above steps for all the remaining scales.

After all the information is transferred from the individual scale record forms, the examiner should record the overall range of scores for stage placements, EDAs, and deviation scores in the spaces provided on the center right-hand section of the Summary Record Form. In addition, the modal stage placement, average EDA, and average deviation scores can be determined as global indices of quantitative performance if so desired, and entered on the Summary Record Form in the spaces provided. (The validity of the EDAs, and the scores derived from them, is presented in Appendix D.) The variability or range in scores that individual children show is used to determine the homogeneous or heterogeneous nature of a child's sensorimotor capabilities. The global indices do not ordinarily enter into the interpretation phase of the clinical-educational process.

Use of the EDA Placements and the Deviation Scores Both of these scores are used to gauge the extent to which a child shows normal, advanced, delayed, or atypical patterns of development. However, it should be remembered that the EDA placements in many cases are esti-

mates of the "modal" age at which children attain the given landmarks. Consequently, caution is warranted in using these age placements and the deviation scores derived from them for purposes other than depicting the child's *current* developmental status. Under no conditions should developmental rates be computed by dividing a given EDA by the child's CA for predictive or other purposes. Sensorimotor development is simply not characterized by a neat linear progression (Uzgiris, 1973). Consequently, the age at which a child acquires a given landmark does not predict the age of acquisition for even a logically established next step in a given developmental sequence (e.g., object permanence), even under normal developmental circumstances (King & Seegmiller, 1973; Lewis & McGurk, 1972; Uzgiris, 1973, 1976a).

Besides this caution, clinicians utilizing the Uzgiris and Hunt scales with handicapped and retarded children should remain aware that the patterns of development among these children often differ qualitatively from those of normal children, even under conditions where both have attained the same developmental level, and consequently have the same EDA placement score. The use of EDA placement scores should therefore be qualified with descriptive information when testing handicapped and retarded children, noting the similarities and/or differences in their responses with respect to normal patterns of development.

At the bottom of the Summary Record Form, space is provided for the examiner to record comments concerning both specific and general aspects of the child's qualitative pattern of sensorimotor development. To enhance an accurate portrayal of the child's sensorimotor capabilities, strengths, weaknesses, and deviations from normal patterns of development, it is recommended that the following information be noted.

1. Record the stage or stages of development in which the child is primarily functioning, and the name of the stage that is characteristic of this level of sensorimotor development. For example, if the child manifested behaviors in Stage III on four of the seven scales, the child's sensorimotor abilities would represent primarily the use of "Secondary Circular Reactions." (The names of the six stages and the characteristics of each are listed in Table 1 above.)
2. Summarize the significance of the behaviors manifested within the primary stage(s) of functioning in language that persons unfamiliar with the Uzgiris and Hunt scales can understand. For example, if the child manifested primarily Stage III abilities, the summary statement might say that the child:

showed the ability to elicit and maintain both sensory and social input and feedback through direct actions on objects and persons. This ability was manifested in the following ways: 1) using an up-and-down hand movement to have the examiner continue producing an interesting popping sound, 2) saying "ah-da" to have the examiner repeat the production of a "da-da" sound, 3) swiping at a roly-poly to elicit auditory and visual feedback from it, and 4) shaking and banging a rattle to produce different sounds that it made.

3. Record the branches of development in which the child is most advanced and most delayed, summarizing the significance of the behaviors manifested. For example, if the child was found to be functioning primarily in Stages II and III, yet achieved Stage IV performance, in, say, object permanence, it might be stated that the child:

> has begun to show the ability to combine and order behaviors required to solve simple problem situations. This ability was shown when the child uncovered a toy in order to secure an object hidden under a screen. This particular response reflected both the child's "memory" of the object once it was covered, and the ability to serialize behaviors in a manner where one behavior served as a means (pulling off the cloth) and another toward obtaining the object (picking up the toy).

4. Record whether the child showed any deviations in his or her pattern of sensorimotor development. Two types of deviations should be noted. First, the attainment of a higher-level landmark while failing to manifest one or more behaviors at the levels immediately below the highest critical behavior achieved should be noted. Quite often, this reflects the acquisition of a "splinter skill" that usually lacks functional utility. Second, any major delays in one or more branches of development should be recorded. For example, if the child is found to be functioning in Stages IV and V in most branches of development, but is found to be functioning in Stage II in, say, vocal imitation, this discrepancy should be noted. To the maximum extent possible, an attempt should be made to identify the variables underlying any major discrepancies in development. Knowledge of such variables can be especially useful when designing intervention procedures. (The child's profile of abilities is particularly helpful for discerning whether or not major discrepancies in development are present—see below.)

If the recommended procedures for recording and summarizing the assessment results have been followed, the clinician should find that the completion of a written report is an easy task.

PROFILING THE CHILD'S SENSORIMOTOR ABILITIES

To provide a graphic representation of the child's sensorimotor abilities, a *Profile of Abilities* form has been constructed so that comparisons can be made between the child's performance levels on the seven scales. The Profile of Abilities form is included in Appendix A.

The achievements comprising the sequential levels of development for each branch have been arranged on the profile form according to the six stages of sensorimotor development. The assignment of sensorimotor achievements to a particular stage of development was made by Piaget (1936, 1937, 1945) on theoretical grounds. According to Piaget, the behaviors comprising the content of a given stage in *all* the separate sensorimotor branches are considered to be particular aspects of a more general cognitive operative process (Flavell, 1963). For example, Stage III behaviors, regardless of the sensorimotor domain, are considered to be manifestations of the secondary circular reaction; that is, attempts to maintain (or reinstate) interesting events produced by the child's own actions. In object permanence, the child attempts to maintain visual contact with objects moving out of the visual field by "searching around the point of an object's disappearance"; in the means-ends area, the child swipes at a roly-poly to maintain the interesting feedback produced; in the genesis of vocal imitation, the child attempts to maintain the production of familiar sounds by imitating the person uttering them, etc.

Given the structural features of the sensorimotor period, one would expect that a child might manifest the same stage performance in all the different sensorimotor branches. However, several lines of evidence indicate that normal infants generally straddle two or more stages in terms of their levels of performance (see Uzgiris, 1976a), and that many severely retarded and organically impaired children often show even greater stage variability (Dunst, 1978b). Such disparities are explained as *horizontal lags* or *decalages* (Piaget, 1973). The term horizontal decalage is used to "...express a chronological difference between the age of acquisition of operations that bear on different concepts (or constructs), but obey identical structural laws...(i.e., emerge through the same stages of development)" (Pinard & Laurendeau, 1969). Thus, although the achievements within a particular sensorimotor stage are structurally related, it can be expected that a child will attain the different landmarks comprising the content of a given stage at different ages.

The usefulness of a sensorimotor profile of abilities is reflected by the fact that horizontal decalages in development occur. A profile provides a graphic representation of a child's overall pattern of sensorimotor development. It portrays the child's range of sensorimotor abilities, and depicts his or her major strengths and weaknesses. A profile of abilities shows the extent to which a child's sensorimotor capabilities are structurally alike, or are representative of quite different sensorimotor skills. In contrast to the data compiled on the Summary Record Form, a profile of abilities provides a different perspective of a child's sensorimotor abilities.

Besides assigning the sequential levels of sensorimotor performance to distinct stages of development on the Profile of Abilities form, the achievements within each stage have been horizontally arranged according to the estimated "modal" age at which the landmarks are ordinarily achieved. Thus, within a given stage, the items that parallel one another horizontally would be expected to be achieved at approximately the same age. Items located toward the lower portion of a stage are those that can ordinarily be expected to be acquired first, whereas the landmarks located toward the upper portion of a stage are ordinarily acquired at a later time.

INTERPRETING THE RESULTS

The information obtained from the recording and profiling process is utilized to determine 1) whether a child is showing delayed or nondelayed sensorimotor performance, 2) whether a child is showing a normal or atypical *pattern* of sensorimotor development, 3) the extent to which discrepancies in development are present, 4) the exact nature of the deviations, if any, and 5) what remedial recommendations are most appropriate for ameliorating the delays and/or deficits manifested. The interpretation or clinical process is concerned specifically with steps 1 through 4, while step 5 falls within the realm of the intervention and educational use of the results.

Before illustrating the implementation of this five-step process, patterns of sensorimotor development that are typical of normal infants are presented to provide the examiner with a reference point for determining whether or not a child is showing a normal or atypical developmental pattern. Four individual cases are presented to illustrate what constitutes normal patterns of development at different points during the sensorimotor period. All four of the children were from middle- to upper-middle-class backgrounds, lived at home, and were participants in a model mother-infant intervention program (Dunst, 1975).

Case A

Beth was 5 months old at the time she was administered the Uzgiris and Hunt scales. She was also administered the Griffiths (1954) Mental Development Scales. She obtained an MA (mental age) of 5.2 months and a GQ (general intelligence quotient) of 104 on the Griffiths test.

The overall findings of the Uzgiris and Hunt assessment (Table A) showed that Beth's EDAs ranged from 3 to 6 months, which yielded deviation scores varying from −2 to +1. Her deviation scores were very close to her actual age, with two scores each falling above and below her CA and three scores showing no deviations.

An examination of Beth's profile of abilities (Figure A) shows that she was functioning in the upper portion of Stage II and the lower portion of Stage III. The major sensorimotor capability manifested was the use of secondary circular reactions. Beth showed the ability to use both social (operational causality—scale step 3c) and nonsocial (e.g., means-ends abilities—scale step 2, and schemes—scale step 4) behaviors to maintain the feedback provided by adults and objects.

The pattern of sensorimotor development exhibited by Beth is very typical of children functioning within the early stages of the sensorimotor period.

Table A. Overall assessment results for Beth (Case A)

Scale	Highest Developmental Attainment	Scale Step	Stage Placement	EDA	Deviation Score
Object Permanence	Lingers at point of object's disappearance	2	II	3	−2
Means-Ends	Secures visually presented objects	4	III	5	0
Vocal Imitation	Vocalizes in response to cooing sounds	3	II	3	−2
Gestural Imitation	Shows positive response to simple gesture	1a	II	6	+1
Causality	Uses procedure—spectacle with no toy	3c	III	5	0
Space	Secures visually presented object	4	III	5	0
Schemes	Simple motor actions: shaking, waving	4	III	6	+1

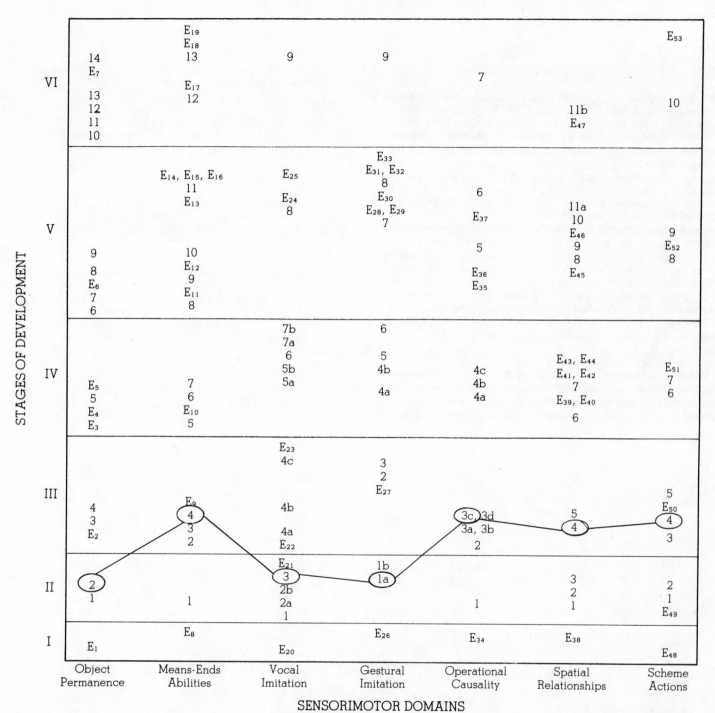

Figure A. Profile of abilities for Beth (Case A).

Case B

The results of an assessment of Marsha, an 8-month-old with an MA of 8.4 months and a GQ of 105, are shown in Table B. An examination of the above results shows that her overall abilities ranged from Stages III to V, with an EDA range from 6 to 10 months. Marsha's deviation scores were nearly symmetrical above and below her CA, the largest deviation being ±2 months.

The profile of abilities depicting Marsha's stage-related performance capabilities (Figure B) shows that, with the exception of achieving Stage V in the means-ends abilities domain, her performance was equally divided between Stages II and III.

Although Marsha's overall pattern of sensorimotor development is generally quite typical, one aspect of her capabilities indicated a minor deviation, although it was not considered an area of concern. Generally, children who have attained Stage IV or V performance in the means-ends abilities domain also perform at a Stage IV or V level in object permanence. However, as can be seen from an examination of Marsha's results, she had not yet manifested the ability either to reverse searching in anticipation of visually locating an object moved behind her back or to obtain an object hidden under a single screen (object permanence—scale steps E_3, E_4, and 5).

The *overall* pattern of development exhibited by Marsha is very typical of infants 8 to 12 months of age. This appears to be a transitional level in the genesis of sensorimotor development, and it therefore is not unusual for a child to straddle three stages, and yet have deviation scores varying only 1 or 2 months from the child's chronological age.

Table B. Overall assessment results for Marsha (Case B)

Scale	Highest Developmental Attainment	Scale Step	Stage Placement	EDA	Deviation Score
Object Permanence	Reverses searching to look for object	4	III	6	−2
Means-Ends	Does not pull support—object held above it	8	V	10	+2
Vocal Imitation	Vocalizes similar sounds—babbling sounds	4b	III	6	−2
Gestural Imitation	Imitates complex gestures/gradual approximation	4a	IV	9	+1
Causality	Touches adult's hands as causal action	4a	IV	10	+2
Space	Reverses bottle to place nipple in mouth	7	IV	9	+1
Schemes	Simple motor actions: shaking, hitting	4	III	6	−2

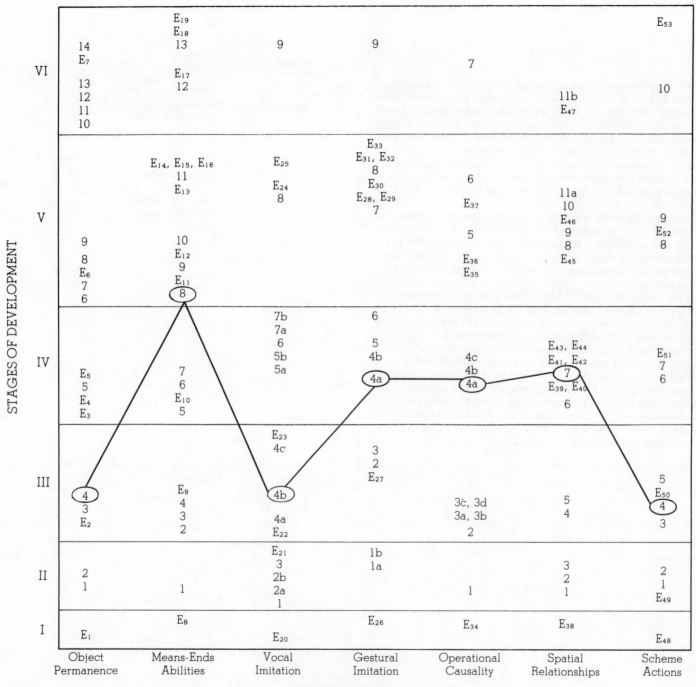

Figure B. Profile of abilities for Marsha (Case B).

Case C

Andrew, when administered the Uzgiris and Hunt scales at the age of 12 months, had an MA of 13.7 months and a GQ of 114. His assessment scores are shown in Table C. Andrew's EDAs varied from 8 to 15 months, and yielded deviation scores ranging from −4 to +3. This is not an unusual range of scores, and in fact is very typical of infants functioning at levels of development toward the second half of the sensorimotor period (Stages IV, V, and VI). Thus, whereas first-year infants generally show deviation from CA scores of about ±1, 2, or 3 months, second-year infants typically show deviations of ±3 or 4 months.

The fact that wider discrepancies are not of concern in infants 12 months of age or older is reflected in Andrew's profile of abilities (Figure C). As can be seen, his sensorimotor capabilities for the most part fell within the upper Stage IV-lower Stage V range. This indicated that his overall performance was much more homogeneous than his deviation scores seemed to show.

Andrew did, however, show an interesting pattern of development that can be seen to contrast sharply with the pattern of development manifested by children showing a delay with regard to the communicative-language aspects of development. In the four areas in which development was most advanced, three concerned themselves with aspects of performance involving relationships between the child and adults. Two of these involve imitation of adult-modeled vocal and gestural behaviors, and the third involved an understanding that an adult could serve as a causal agent toward obtaining some desired goal (operational causality—scale step 5). Generally, children who have language deficits are often quite delayed in these areas of performance relative to development in the other sensorimotor domains.

Table C. Overall assessment results for Andrew (Case C)

Scale	Highest Developmental Attainment	Scale Step	Stage Placement	EDA	Deviation Score
Object Permanence	Secures object/one screen/ visible displacement	5	IV	8	−4
Means-Ends	Pulls object up from floor using string	10	V	13	+1
Vocal Imitation	Imitates familiar words	5b	IV	12	0
Gestural Imitation	Imitates unfamiliar, visible gestures	6	IV	15	+3
Causality	Gives toy to adult as causal action	5	V	14	+2
Space	Turns doll over to view face	7	IV	9	−3
Schemes	Drops object/follows trajectory	7	IV	10	−2

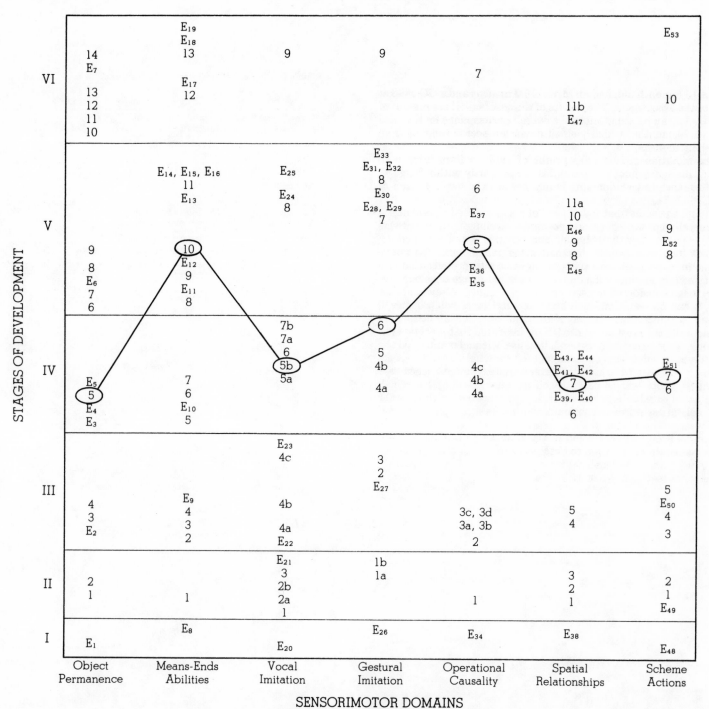

Figure C. Profile of abilities for Andrew (Case C).

Case D

Michael, a 16.5-month-old, had an MA of 16.2 months and a GQ of 98 at the time of the assessment. The results of the assessment are presented in Table D. As can be seen, Michael's overall performance level varied from 12 to 20 months, which yielded deviation scores ranging from −4.5 to +3.5 months.

An examination of Michael's profile of abilities form (Figure D) shows that his sensorimotor capabilities fell primarily within Stage V, with performance in two domains falling toward the lower portion of Stage VI.

Although the somewhat lower level of performance in vocal imitation is generally not typical among normally developing infants, it was reported by the mother that Michael not only possessed a limited vocabulary of functional words, but had never readily imitated adult-modeled sounds. By itself, this pattern might be interpreted as indicating that this child manifested a deficit in vocal-language development. However, when considered in relation to performance in several other domains, it can be seen that such an interpretation is not warranted. First of all, the fact that Michael's gestural imitation abilities were developmentally the most advanced (EDA) indicated that imitation per se was not an area of concern. Second, because Michael manifested the abilities to use an adult as a causal agent (operational causality—scale step 5) and to use objects to instigate interactive exchanges (schemes—scale step 9), there was apparently no deficit regarding his social-communicative capabilities. Moreover, it was reported by the mother that Michael did use words to communicate, but he simply had a limited vocabulary.

As can be seen, interpretation of the findings in a given domain should be considered in relation to both performance in other branches of development and supplemental information, including parental reports and other test data when available.

Table D. Overall assessment results for Michael (Case D)

Scale	Highest Developmental Attainment	Scale Step	Stage Placement	EDA	Deviation Score
Object Permanence	Secures object/invisible displ./three screens	12	VI	15	−1.5
Means-Ends	Pulls object up from floor using string	10	V	13	−3.5
Vocal Imitation	Imitates familiar words	5b	IV	12	−4.5
Gestural Imitation	Imitates one invisible gesture	8	V	20	+3.5
Causality	Attempts to activate toy following demonstration	6	V	18	+1.5
Space	Makes complex detour to obtain object	E$_{47}$	VI	18	+1.5
Schemes	Shows objects to mother	9	V	15	−1.5

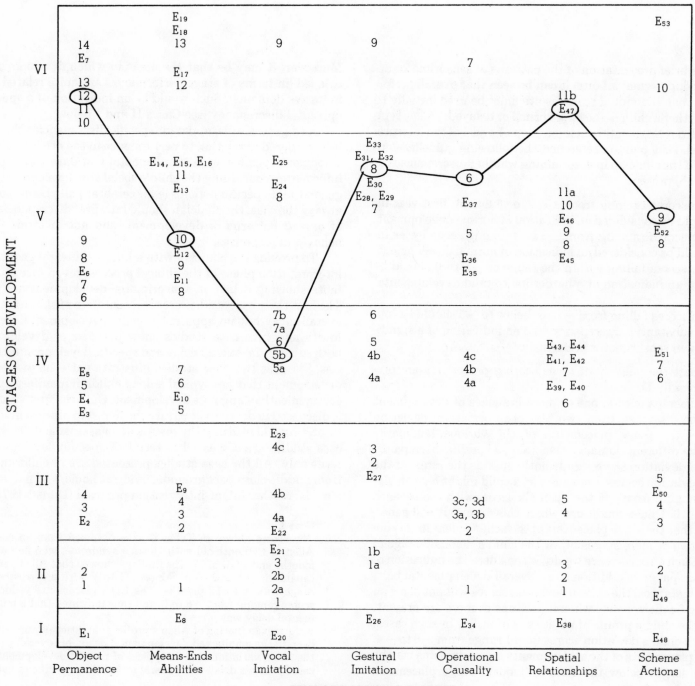

Figure D. Profile of abilities for Michael (Case D).

From this brief presentation of the patterns of sensorimotor development among normal infants, it can be seen that overall performance rather than individual scale results must be used initially to determine whether a child is showing normal or delayed, and/or typical or atypical, developmental patterns (steps 1 and 2 of the interpretation process). As a point of reference, the following guidelines are provided to aid the clinician in determining whether discrepancies in development are present.

1. Deviation scores ranging from ±1, 2, or 3 among first-year infants should be considered an indication of normal development.
2. Deviation scores ranging from ±3 or 4 among second-year infants should be considered an indication of normal development.
3. Deviation scores falling within the range of −6 to 0 should be considered an indication of a borderline to mild developmental delay.
4. Deviation scores falling from −10 or below to −5 should be considered a substantial discrepancy, and an indication of a significant delay in sensorimotor performance.

Data to support the validity of these scoring procedures are presented in Appendix D.

Specific discrepancies in one or more branches of development can usually be discerned from two bits of information: deviation scores and/or the stage placements of the various landmarks achieved in the different domains. Generally, a specific discrepancy will produce a deviation score significantly outside the range of the majority of deviation scores. For example, a child might have deviation scores ranging from −5 to −1 in six areas, with the seventh score being −10. Under conditions where this occurs, it will generally be found that the stage placement of the achievement in this domain will be two or more stages below the child's "modal" stage of functioning. Such an occurrence would be considered an indication of a specific discrepancy in addition to an overall developmental lag.

In many instances, the child's deviation scores will not show an apparent specific discrepancy when in fact one or more are present. The form of the child's profile of abilities is of utility in such cases. For example, a child's deviation scores might range from −8 to −4, but the stage placements of the achievements in two domains may be two or more stages below the child's "modal" stage placement.

Moreover, it may be that the areas in which development is most delayed (in terms of stage performance) are quite related (e.g., both imitative domains). Such would be an indication of a specific developmental discrepancy (see Cases H and I below).

As a general rule, apparent specific discrepancies should always be considered in relation to performance in the other branches of development together with supplemental test data and supplemental information concerning the child's social and developmental history, general and specific deficits (e.g., cerebral palsy), and so on. As is always the case, the clinician should interpret discrepancies in terms of *overall* patterns of development, and not in terms of isolated behavioral responses.

To provide the clinician with additional insights concerning the interpretation phase of the clinical process, seven case studies of infants showing delays in sensorimotor development are presented. The first three case studies are representative of children showing an overall delay but no apparent specific developmental deficits. The fourth and fifth case studies show patterns of development with both substantial overall delay and specific developmental discrepancies. The last two case studies illustrate patterns of sensorimotor development that are typical among children manifesting delays in communicative-language development. Only the first study, Case E, is discussed in detail to illustrate the five-step process involved in interpreting and utilizing the results of an assessment. The remaining case studies are discussed in terms of specific developmental patterns only. All the case studies presented are of children who were from middle-class backgrounds, living at home, and participating in a model mother-infant intervention program (Dunst, 1975).

Case E

The scores shown in Table E were obtained from an assessment of Allen, a 12-month-old with Down's syndrome, who had an MA of 12 months and a GQ of 77. The findings showed that Allen's sensorimotor capabilities ranged from Stages III to V with a corresponding EDA range from 6 to 12 months. The EDA placements yielded deviation scores ranging from −6 to 0, and thus indicated that a minor developmental delay was present.

An examination of Allen's profile of abilities (Figure E) shows that despite the manifested developmental delay, his overall pattern shows the same variation that is typical of normal development. This indicated that his delay was general rather than specific in nature.

Table E. Overall assessment results for Allen (Case E)

Scale	Highest Developmental Attainment	Scale Step	Stage Placement	EDA	Deviation Score
Object Permanence	Secures object/visible disp./one screen	5	IV	8	−4
Means-Ends	Pulls string horizontally to obtain toy	9	V	11	−1
Vocal Imitation	Imitates familiar babbling sounds	5a	IV	12	0
Gestural Imitation	Attempts to imitate complex gestures	3	III	8	−4
Causality	Touches object as causal action	4b	IV	10	−2
Space	Follows object falling within view	5	III	6	−6
Schemes	Uses complex motor actions: hits blocks	6	IV	9	−3

The results showed that Allen was functioning primarily in Stage IV, and thus his sensorimotor skills were representative of the ability to coordinate secondary circular reactions. In other words, Allen was able to order behaviors in goal-directed sequences where one behavior served as the means (or tool) toward obtaining a desired goal. Among the Stage IV behaviors manifested, Allen was able to remove a cloth to obtain a toy hidden under it, imitate babbling sounds that he ordinarily produced, touch an object (after the examiner produced an interesting spectacle with it) as a causal behavior to have the spectacle repeated, and apply various complex motor actions (e.g., hitting objects together, sliding, tearing) to different toys and materials. As a total pattern of development, Allen's responses showed that he had begun to understand that his actions, in response to different problem-solving and "game" situations, had the effect of producing a predetermined result (e.g., obtaining an object by removing a cloth placed over it). Moreover, the fact that Stage IV was attained in two domains involving knowledge of objects (object permanence and schemes) and in two domains involving knowledge of relationships between himself and other persons (vocal imitation and operational causality) indicated that both general and social sensorimotor abilities had been acquired simultaneously.

Allen's major strength was in the means-ends abilities domain, where he pulled a string along a horizontal surface to obtain a toy attached to it. This indicated that Allen not only understood the relationship between the string and toy attached to it, but also his role as an agent in using the string as a tool.

Allen's major weakness was in the spatial relationship area, where he manifested the ability to follow the trajectory of an object dropped from above his head that fell within view, but did not locate the terminal position of an object falling outside the visual field. This inability was, in part, a result of poor head and upper torso control. Each time Allen attempted to search for the dropped object, he would start to fall toward the side the object was dropped, and then right himself rather than continue looking for the object. Thus, motor immaturity rather than a sensorimotor deficit apparently underscored this developmental weakness.

It would be tempting to implicate motor immaturity as the reason Allen did not imitate complex motor actions composed of familiar schemes (scale step 5). Although this may in part have underscored this inability, it was clearly not the major explanation. This was the case because, on the scheme scale, Allen did manifest various complex motor actions with toys. Thus, his inability to approximate or imitate adult-modeled complex gestures appeared to be a result of his failure to be able to realize that he had to modify his own actions and not simply repeat any behavior in response to what the examiner did.

The results of this assessment led to both specific and general recommendations designed to utilize existing behavioral skills to foster development in the areas in which interventions were considered to be needed (object permanence, gestural imitation, and spatial relationships). The rationale for consolidating and integrating activities into *intervention packages* is presented in the last part of this section.

The first intervention package prescribed for Allen integrated object permanence, means-ends abilities, spatial relationships, and schemes for relating to objects. For example, one activity had Allen seated on the floor with a bucket about 8 inches high placed between his legs. The container was filled about half-way with different toys that tended to elicit behaviors (scheme actions) already manifested by Allen. In playing with Allen, the mother was instructed to occasionally drop toys in and to the side of the bucket, and eventually behind the bucket to elicit searching behaviors from Allen. Although quite simple, this activity developed the ability to search both for objects falling out of view (spatial relationships—scale step 6) and for objects disappearing in various locations (object permanence—scale steps E_5, 6, and 7). As part of this activity, objects attached to strings were also placed in the bucket and covered with a piece of paper or cloth to foster integrated means-ends—object permanence abilities.

A second intervention package integrated behaviors in the vocal imitation, gestural imitation, operational causality, and schemes for relating to objects domains into an activity sequence. A series of simple and complex motor behaviors already manifested by Allen were first identified. As part of this activity, the mother was instructed that, rather than simply give toys to Allen to play with, she should demonstrate (model) a behavior that he habitually applied to a given toy to instigate a my turn–your turn sequence. Simple motor actions were initially presented, then gradually modified, requiring Allen to more closely approximate the modeled behaviors in order to be reinforced.

As part of the above mother-child play episode, the mother was also instructed to occasionally model novel behaviors or actions to elicit causal behaviors from Allen that indicated that he wanted her to repeat the interesting spectacles. Also, when presenting several motor actions, vocalizations were paired with the different motor actions, and produced in a repetitious manner to elicit simultaneous vocal-gestural imitation. For example, when patting a drum, the sound "boom-boom" was produced with each patting action. Several different vocal-gestural actions were presented in this manner to facilitate integrated vocal-gestural imitation abilities.

As can be seen from this brief description of several examples of the intervention packages actually developed, the focus of the play episode shifted back and forth between different sensorimotor skills, facilitating not only specific targeted behaviors, but also the ability to have Allen shift his attention to various aspects of the toys, the actions produced, his mother's behavior, and his own behavior in relation to the nature of the problem-solving tasks presented. Uzgiris (1976a) considers the ability to "modify one's behavior by differentiated feedback" as a major attainment in the acquisition of sensorimotor intelligence. Facilitating this ability represents one major goal for children functioning primarily in Stage IV of the sensorimotor period (see "Guidelines for Developing Intervention Activities" below).

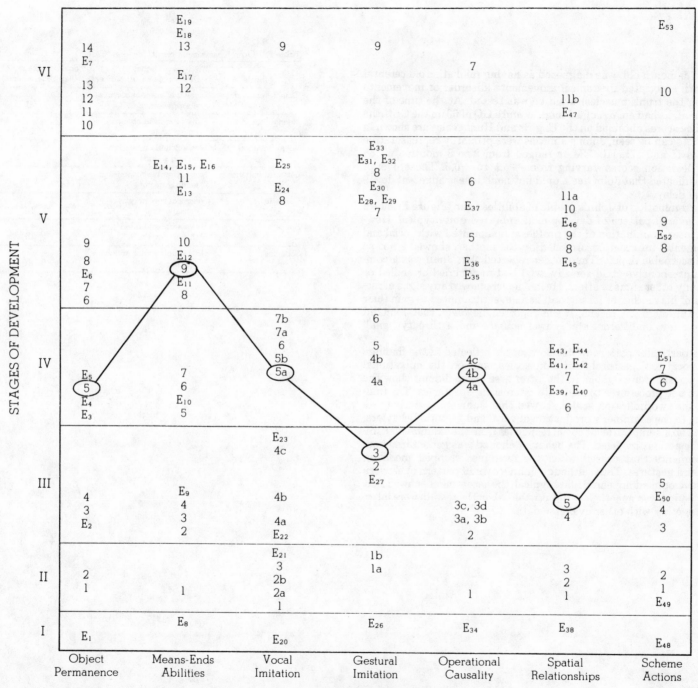

Figure E. Profile of abilities for Allen (Case E).

Case F

John, a 7.5-month-old, was diagnosed as having mild athetoid cerebral palsy with associated dystonical movements (disorder of movements involving the trunk muscles) when he was tested. At the time of the assessment, he had an MA of 4.8 months and a GQ of 63 on the Griffiths scales. The scores obtained on the Uzgiris and Hunt scales are shown in Table F. As can be seen, John's abilities were primarily representative of Stages II and III. His EMAs ranged from 2 to 8 months, which yielded deviation scores varying from −5.5 to +0.5. These overall results indicated that John has a mild but nonetheless apparent developmental delay.

An examination of John's profile of abilities form (Figure F) shows that his overall pattern of development appeared quite typical. However, a closer examination of the profile, supplemented with social and developmental information provided by the mother, showed a not so easily discernable deficit. The mother reported that John was a completely unresponsive child socially, who had never cried or smiled or showed any other signs of affect. He had never showed any signs of recognition of his mother or father, and had never attempted to gain their attention through any means. It was reported, however, that John did produce a few undifferentiated vowel sounds and a throaty "gaa" sound.

This particular pattern of development is reflected in the findings on the vocal and gestural imitation scales, and on the operational causality scale. For example, in the latter area, John did not show the ability to use procedures to reinstate interesting spectacles. The findings on the two imitation scales showed that John was primarily responding to the examiner's production of vocal and gestural behaviors, but made no attempt to elicit social responses from the examiner by imitating the actions modeled. The behavior elicited was generalized bodily movements that ceased when the examiner stopped modeling sounds and gestures. Thus, although John's overall pattern of sensorimotor development appeared quite typical, the assessment showed that a major deficit was nonetheless discernable when the results were interpreted together with other available data.

Table F.   Overall assessment results for John (Case F)

Scale	Highest Developmental Attainment	Scale Step	Stage Placement	EDA	Deviation Score
Object Permanence	Lingers at point of object's disappearance	2	II	3	−4.5
Means-Ends	Pulls support to obtain object on it	6	IV	8	+0.5
Vocal Imitation	Gets excited on hearing cooing sounds	2a	II	2	−5.5
Gestural Imitation	Shows positive response to familiar gesture	1a	II	6	−1.5
Causality	Swipes at roly-poly as causal action	2	III	3	−4.5
Space	Follows object falling within view	5	III	6	−1.5
Schemes	Uses simple motor actions: shaking	4	III	6	−1.5

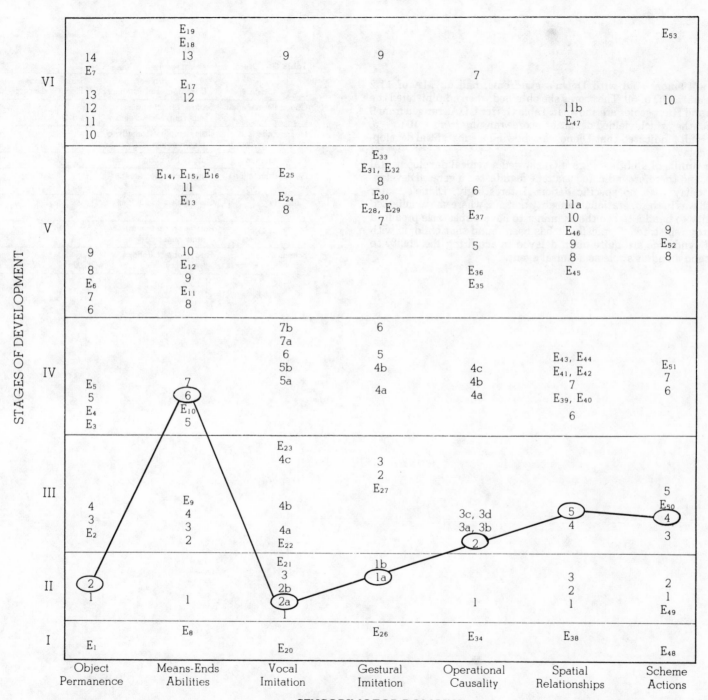

Figure F. Profile of abilities for John (Case F).

Case G

Diane, a 19-month-old with Down's syndrome, had an MA of 11.2 months and a GQ of 59. The scores she obtained when administered the Uzgiris and Hunt scales are shown in Table G. Her EDAs ranged from 9 to 14 months, which yielded deviation scores ranging from −10 to −5. These results indicated that Diane was showing a substantial developmental delay.

Her profile of abilities (Figure G) showed a typical developmental pattern, and therefore indicated that she manifested a general developmental delay with no specific deficit. Interestingly, Diane's major strength was in the operational causality domain, where she manifested the ability to hand a toy to the examiner to have a spectacle produced by the toy reinstated. Typically, it has been found that children with Down's syndrome are quite often delayed in acquiring the ability to understand an adult's role as a causal agent.

Table G. Overall assessment results for Diane (Case G)

Scale	Highest Developmental Attainment	Scale Step	Stage Placement	EDA	Deviation Score
Object Permanence	Secures object under superimposed screens	8	V	10	−9
Means-Ends	Uses string horizontally to obtain object	9	V	11	−8
Vocal Imitation	Imitates babbling sounds	5a	IV	12	−7
Gestural Imitation	Imitates complex familiar gestures	5	IV	12	−7
Causality	Gives object to adult as causal action	5	V	14	−5
Space	Rotates object to view functional side	7	IV	9	−10
Schemes	Throws objects/follows trajectory	7	IV	10	−9

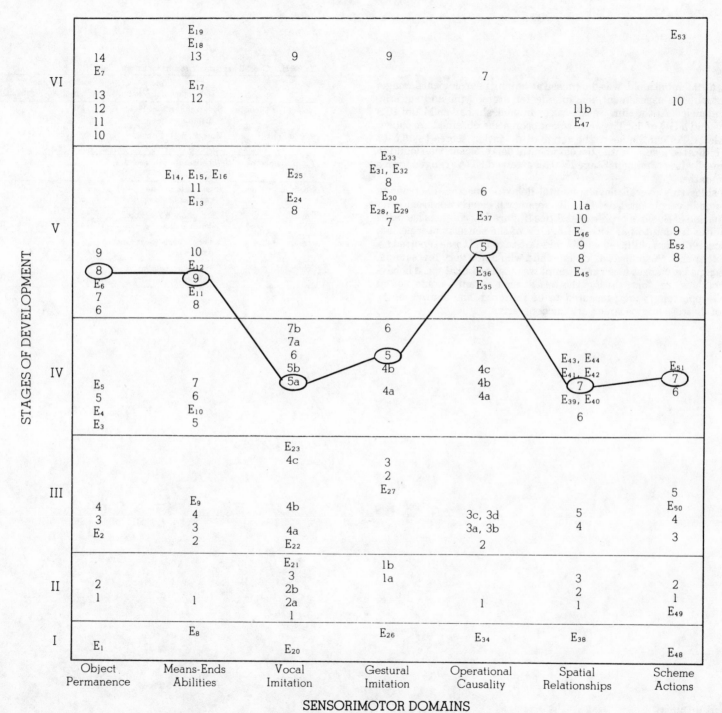

Figure G. Profile of abilities for Diane (Case G).

Case H

Susan, a 19.5-month-old, was diagnosed as having neurological damage. Throughout the assessment, she manifested stereotypic and autistic-like tendencies. At the time Susan was examined, she had an MA of 10.8 months and a GQ of 55. The assessment scores she obtained are shown in Table H. As can be seen, the range of deviation scores (−16.5 to −9.5) indicated a substantial developmental delay. Susan was found to be primarily functioning in Stage IV. Her attained EDAs ranged from 3 to 10 months.

Besides this overall developmental delay, a specific discrepancy was found in vocal imitation. This discrepancy is clearly apparent in an examination of Susan's profile of abilities (Figure H). Whereas her overall abilities tended to fall within Stage IV of the sensorimotor period, her vocal imitation skills fell within middle Stage II. It was reported by the mother that Susan was a "quiet" child who made very few sounds, and became very upset when an attempt was made to elicit vocal behaviors from her. In fact, during the assessment, when sounds not in Susan's repertoire were presented to be imitated, she showed overt signs of distress and became very uncooperative.

Table H. Overall assessment results for Susan (Case H)

Scale	Highest Developmental Attainment	Scale Step	Stage Placement	EDA	Deviation Score
Object Permanence	Secures object/visible disp./one screen	5	IV	8	−11.5
Means-Ends	Uses support to obtain object placed on it	6	IV	8	−11.5
Vocal Imitation	Vocalizes in response to cooing sounds	3	II	3	−16.5
Gestural Imitation	Attempts to imitate complex gestures	3	III	8	−11.5
Causality	Touches adult's hand as causal action	4a	IV	10	−9.5
Space	Rotates objects/views functional side	7	IV	9	−10.5
Schemes	Throws objects/follows trajectory	7	IV	10	−9.5

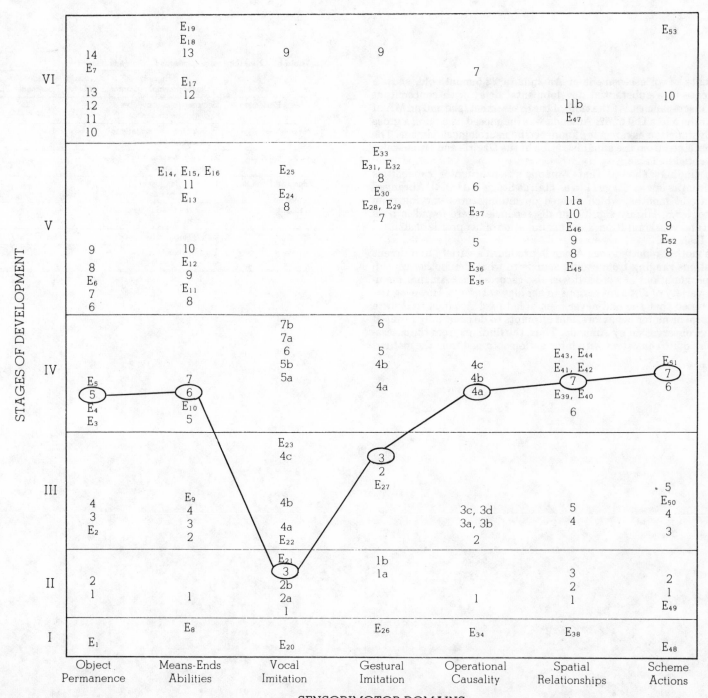

Figure H. Profile of abilities for Susan (Case H).

Case I

The results of an assessment of Amanda, a 22.5-month-old, show a classic case of a substantial developmental delay with concomitant specific discrepancies. At the time of the assessment, she had an MA of 11.7 months and a GQ of 52. Amanda was diagnosed as having a gross motor dysfunction as a result of nonspecific neurological damage. The scores obtained from the administration of the Uzgiris and Hunt scales are presented in Table I.

The findings showed that Amanda's sensorimotor capabilities ranged from as low as Stage II to as high as Stage V. Her EDAs ranged from 2 to 14 months, which yielded deviation scores varying from −20.5 to −8.5. Highly significant discrepancies were found in both gestural and vocal imitation, as an examination of her profile of abilities (Figure I) shows.

The mother reported that Amanda produced a variety of different vocalizations ranging from cooing sounds to what the mother considered approximations of words. It was also reported that Amanda manifested a variety of different actions in her play with toys. However, the mother noted that she had never been able to get Amanda to imitate either vocal or motor behaviors, and attempts to do so usually resulted in passive observation by Amanda. Thus, the findings from the assessment were quite consistent with information obtained from the mother.

Table I. Overall assessment results for Amanda (Case I)

Scale	Highest Developmental Attainment	Scale Step	Stage Placement	EDA	Deviation Score
Object Permanence	Secures object/invisible disp./one screen	9	V	13	−9.5
Means-Ends	Pulls string horizontally to obtain object	9	V	11	−11.5
Vocal Imitation	Smiles in response to cooing sounds	2a	II	2	−20.5
Gestural Imitation	Bangs table on seeing familiar gesture	1b	II	7	−15.5
Causality	Gives toy to adult as causal action	5	V	14	−8.5
Space	Builds tower of two cubes	9	V	14	−8.5
Schemes	Throws objects/follows trajectory	7	IV	10	−12.5

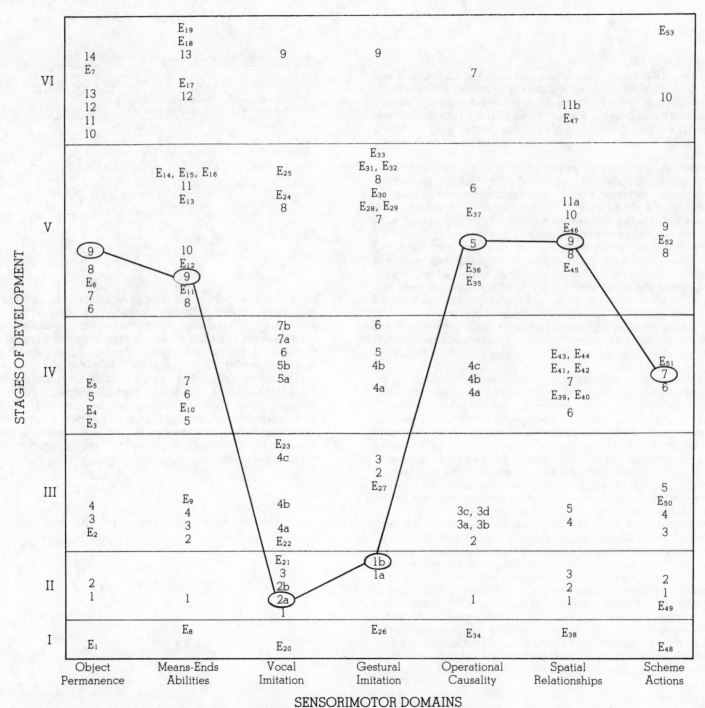

Figure I. Profile of abilities for Amanda (Case I).

Case J

Anne, a 16-month-old with spina bifida, had an MA of 12.7 months and a GQ of 79 at the time of the assessment. The assessment scores obtained are shown in Table J. The findings showed that Anne's sensorimotor abilities were all within Stages IV and V. Her EDAs ranged from 9 to 14 months, which yielded deviation scores varying from -7 to -2. These results indicated that Anne was manifesting a mild developmental delay.

An examination of Anne's profile of abilities (Figure J) indicates that her overall pattern shows the same variability that is typical of normal development. However, a closer examination of specific aspects of her sensorimotor abilities shows that her pattern of development is characteristic of children manifesting a specific delay with regard to the social-communicative aspects of language.

Besides the child's motor disability resulting from spina bifida, the mother's major concern regarding Anne's development was her lack of any functional language. It was reported that Anne "jabbered" constantly, but that she never used sounds to communicate desires, protest, etc. or to label objects or persons. Furthermore, it was reported that Anne was primarily "taken care of" by her six older siblings who "did everything for her." The mother indicated that she believed one reason Anne did not talk was because her brothers and sisters "anticipated her needs" and never gave her a chance to "do anything for herself."

Several recent lines of investigation concerning the relationship between sensorimotor development and linguistic competence (see "Guidelines for Developing Intervention Activities" below) have found that Stage V performance may be a necessary condition before functional language abilities are manifested. Moreover, Stage V performance in sensorimotor domains that are *socially* oriented have been implicated as the prerequisite for the communicative aspects of language, whereas Stage V sensorimotor abilities, which are more indicative of the child's *knowledge* of the permanence of objects and the relationships between objects, have been implicated as the precursors for the semantic aspects of language.

An examination of Anne's profile of abilities shows that the three areas in which she is functioning at Stage IV are the socially oriented domains. Functioning at or below Stage IV in vocal imitation, gestural imitation, and operational causality concomitant with Stage V or above performance in the remaining domains has been found to be very typical among children lacking functional language abilities, and is generally characteristic of a specific delay with regard to the social-communicative aspects of language. Although children manifesting such a pattern do communicate, quite often the mode of communication is infantile (e.g., crying, "grunting"). In contrast, children functioning at or above Stage V in the socially oriented domains of the Uzgiris and Hunt scales generally use objects to gain an adult's attention (schemes—

Table J. Overall assessment results for Anne (Case J)

Scale	Highest Developmental Attainment	Scale Step	Stage Placement	EDA	Deviation Score
Object Permanence	Secures object/visible disp./three screens	7	V	9	−7
Means-Ends	Pulls string horizontally to obtain object	9	V	11	−5
Vocal Imitation	Imitates babbling sounds	5	IV	12	−4
Gestural Imitation	Imitates complex gestures by gradual approx.	4a	IV	9	−7
Causality	Touches adult's hands as causal action	4	IV	10	−6
Space	Builds tower of two cubes	9	V	14	−2
Schemes	Socially instigated actions— inanimate objects	8	V	13	−3

scale step 9) and/or use an adult as an intervening agent toward some goal (operational causality—scale step 5). Moreover, vocalizations often accompany gestural acts (operational causality—scale step E_{37}), and eventually vocalizations tend to be used more and more as communicative behaviors (vocal imitation—scale steps E_{24}, E_{25}, and 9; spatial relationships—scale step 11b; schemes—scale Step 10).

Whenever a child shows a pattern of development similar to that of Case J, it should be considered a possible indication of a specific delay with regard to the social-communicative aspects of development. In such instances, further assessment of the child's communicative and linguistic abilities should be made. Moreover, an intervention package should be specifically developed to facilitate more appropriate communicative behaviors.

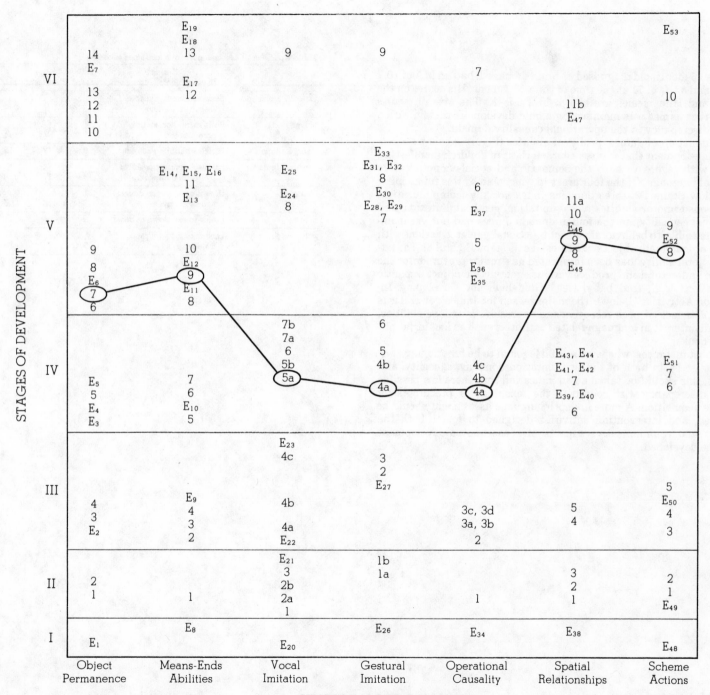

Figure J. Profile of abilities for Anne (Case J).

Case K

James, a 15-month-old diagnosed as brain damaged, had an MA of 10.7 months and a GQ of 71 at the time of the assessment. His scores on the Uzgiris and Hunt scales are shown in Table K. The overall results showed that James was manifesting a mild developmental lag, with a specific discrepancy in the operational causality domain.

Examination of James' profile of abilities (Figure K) shows a pattern of development that is often characteristic of children manifesting a delay with regard to both the semantic and social-communicative aspects of language. Of the four areas in which James was functioning at or below Stage IV, three domains index socially (communicative) related sensorimotor abilities (vocal imitation, gestural imitation, and operational causality); in the fourth domain James had not yet manifested the ability to behaviorally enact functionally related actions with animate or inanimate objects (schemes—scale steps E_{51} and 8). The latter behavioral ability has been implicated as a major precursor for the ability to understand and produce various agent-action-object semantic constructions (e.g., feed baby) (see "Guidelines for Developing Intervention Activities" below). The major reason for James' referral was his complete lack of both receptive and expressive language abilities, and his disinterest in language-related activities such as looking at pictures in books.

In most instances, whenever a child is found to be functioning at or below Stage IV in both of the two imitation domains, causality, and schemes, this should be taken as an indication that there is a possible specific discrepancy with regard to the sensorimotor precursors for language acquisition. A more in-depth language assessment should be conducted, and intervention activities designed to foster both the semantic and communicative aspects of sensorimotor development should be developed.

Table K. Overall assessment results for James (Case K)

Scale	Highest Developmental Attainment	Scale Step	Stage Placement	EDA	Deviation Score
Object Permanence	Secures object/invisible disp./two screens	6	V	9	−6
Means-Ends	Pulls string horizontally to obtain object	9	V	11	−4
Vocal Imitation	Imitates babbling sounds	5a	IV	12	−3
Gestural Imitation	Imitates complex gestures by gradual approx.	4a	IV	9	−6
Causality	Uses procedures as causal action/no toy	3c	III	5	−10
Space	Builds tower of two cubes	9	V	14	−1
Schemes	Throws objects/follows trajectory	7	IV	10	−5

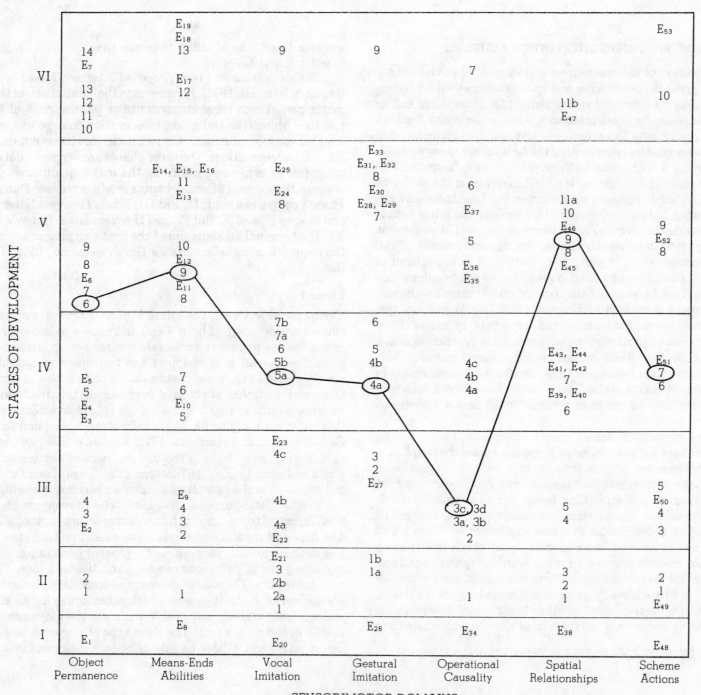

Figure K. Profile of abilities for James (Case K).

GUIDELINES FOR DEVELOPING INTERVENTION ACTIVITIES[2]

In this final section of the manual, several suggested guidelines are presented to provide the clinician and interventionist with a framework for utilizing the results of an assessment for educational and intervention purposes. In most instances, when assessment findings are used for prescribing intervention activities, it is recommended that the assessment item representing the first failure along a particular developmental continuum be "designated" as a "targeted" behavior to be taught. For example, if a child manifested the ability to secure an object hidden under a single screen but failed to secure the same object when hidden under one of two screens, the latter behavior would generally be targeted as an intervention goal. A somewhat different approach is advocated herein for several reasons. First, when development along a particular continuum is considered in isolation, no explicit consideration is given to the relationships that exist between the achievements that comprise the content of the various sensorimotor domains (see Uzgiris, 1973, 1976a). Second, specific achievements are often considered important in and of themselves rather than as particular aspects of a more general cognitive developmental process. Third, where specific achievements are "targeted" as intervention behaviors to be taught, no consideration is given to the functionality of the "skills" facilitated. Under such conditions, test training rather than concept development appears to have occurred.

The above curriculum design considerations (or, more exactly, shortcomings) have led the author to propose a model that explicitly views the attainments of the sensorimotor period as particular "building blocks" for subsequent cognitive-linguistic development (Dunst, in preparation). Rather than being viewed as isolated developmental occurrences, the attainments comprising the content of each of the seven sensorimotor domains explicated by Uzgiris and Hunt (1975) are considered to be specific manifestations of a more general developmental process. In other words, explicit consideration is given to the interrelationships between the contents of the different domains where already manifested behaviors are used as a basis for fostering development in other branches of development. Moreover, the behaviors are taught within the context where they

_____
[2]The material presented in this section is abstracted from Dunst (in preparation).

would ordinarily be of utility to ensure that the skills taught become functional and adaptive.

The model that has been proposed is termed *Phase Intervention* (Dunst & Brassell, 1975). It represents the subdivision of the sensorimotor period into three components or phases, each of which has specified objectives and goals, intervention frameworks, and guidelines for implementation of the recommended intervention activities (Dunst, in preparation). The three phases are derived from and based on empirical evidence concerning the major qualitative shifts that occur in the genesis of sensorimotor intelligence (see Dunst, 1978a). Phase I covers Stages I, II, and III; Phase II covers latter Stage III and Stages IV and V; and Phase III covers latter Stage V and Stage VI. The terminal attainments of the first two phases are considered the requisite entry behaviors for the subsequent phase of intervention.

Phase I

The major objective of the Phase I intervention procedures is to facilitate a wide range of both social and nonsocial behaviors that the infant can use to gain and maintain control over external receptor inputs. The overall goal of Phase I is to transform the infant from simply a *passive* recipient of stimulation to an *active* seeker, manipulator, and controller of external environmental (stimuli) inputs. The secondary circular reaction (i.e., Stage III achievements) represents this latter ability. The Phase I attainments correspond to what McCall, Hogarty, and Hurlburt (1972) have identified as the "perceptual contingency" level in the development of sensorimotor intelligence and what Uzgiris (1976a) terms the "level of simple undifferential actions" in the overall genesis of sensorimotor intelligence.

For heuristic purposes, five categories of response classes have been targeted to be taught. None, however, are mutually exclusive. The first and most common response class involves *manual* activities such as pulling, swiping, hitting, batting, shaking, and squeezing, using visually directed reaching abilities as a means to control receptor inputs. The second category of secondary circular reactions are *non-manual* activities where such behaviors as leg kicking or generalized body activity are used to maintain the movement of, say, a mobile in the child's crib. The third type of response category typifies what Piaget (1937) has described as magico-phenomenalistic causality (operational causality—scale steps 3a, 3b, 3c, and 3d). For intervention purposes, the activities in this response class have been termed *artificial* contingency (Watson, 1966) games (e.g., "nibbling" on the child's neck following head rotation from side to side) inasmuch as the reinforcing stimuli is mediated by an adult. The fourth response class exemplifies situations where *social* responses (e.g., smiling, laughing, and "recognition" behaviors) are used to initiate, reinstate, and/or maintain social encounters between the child and his/her caregivers. The last response category facilitated includes *vocal* behaviors that the infant can use to initiate and sustain child-adult interactions (e.g., using a cooing sound to maintain adult attention).

The basic premise underlying the intervention procedures of Phase I is that secondary circular reactions emerge from and build on the early adaptations the infant makes to environmental encounters (Stage I and II attainments). It is therefore important that the child have a broad behavioral edifice of reflex, sensory, and motoric responses that can be used to develop secondary circular reactions (see Campbell, 1974; Didoha & Dunst, 1975; Dunst, in preparation). Once such an edifice is developed, activities designed to foster secondary circular reactions can be introduced. It is recommended that 1) at least three to five different behaviors within *each* category of secondary circular reactions be fostered, 2) the same behavior (e.g., visually directed reaching) be used in different categories (e.g., manually swiping at a mobile, touching an adult's mouth to be kissed) to foster generalization, and 3) whenever possible, the activities be implemented during ongoing, naturalistic encounters between the child and objects and persons in the environment, rather than under highly structured, artificial learning situations. This ensures that the behaviors facilitated become functional and adaptive.

An examination of the case studies presented above shows that Cases A and F would have activities prescribed that were primarily designed to facilitate secondary circular reactions. As part of their intervention packages, both Cases H and I above would also have activities designed to facilitate Stage III indicative behaviors in the imitation domains. The procedure used would be to identify already manifested behaviors and have them modeled for the child while concomitantly pairing vocal patterns with the actions to foster reciprocal imitation between the child and his teacher and/or parent (see Case E above).

Phase II

The major objective of Phase II of the intervention procedures is to develop behaviors that are characteristic of what Uzgiris (1976a) terms the "level of regulation by differentiated feedback" in the genesis of sensorimotor intelligence. These are behaviors that reflect not only the infant's ability to modify his/her actions based on their outcomes, but are also actions that reflect the infant's recognition of two or more sequences as alternatives, yet equivalent, ways of arriving at a desired terminus (Berlyne, 1970). The ability to modify one's behavior to secure a toy displaced under a chair following several unsuccessful attempts to reach directly for it represents the former behavior, whereas recognizing "extending the arms out to be picked up," "showing" objects, and "calling to" an adult as equivalent ways to initiate interactive exchanges represents the latter ability. The ability to engage in these types of sensorimotor acts is characteristic of what Piaget (1936) considers Stage V attainments of the sensorimotor period.

The overall goal of Phase II is to develop "regulated differentiated feedback" behaviors that are considered to be the precursors for representational problem-solving (Berlyne, 1965, 1970; Piaget, 1936, 1937), symbolic play (Piaget, 1945), the semantic aspects of language (Brown, 1973; Edmonds, 1976; Edwards, 1973; Leonard, 1976), and the communicative aspects of language (Bates, 1976; Dunst, 1978c; Leonard, 1976; Moerk, 1977; Sugarman, 1978). The behaviors facilitated in Phase II are considered the essential "building blocks" for the ability to acquire symbolically based functional language skills; that is, language that involves the use of words as *signifiers* for perceptually absent objects, events, and so forth and that is *semantically* organized and used for *communicative* purposes. The Phase II attainments correspond to the level of sensorimotor development that McCall et al. (1972) consider to be a transitional stage between simple motor learning and subsequent cognitive-verbal learning.

The intervention activities for Phase II are arranged according to the individual branches of development, but, as for Phase I, this has been done primarily for heuristic purposes. In the actual implementation of the intervention activities, every effort should be made to ensure the integration of attainments across the different domains. For example, if the child were being taught to open a jar to remove its contents and to imitate unfamiliar sound patterns (both Stage V attainments), the teacher might model opening the jar while concomitantly uttering the sound "uh-um" as if the vocal *commenting* were necessary in order to open the container (see Case E above for intervention activities).

It has been found useful to think about the attainments of Stages IV and V as being *psychological, psychosocial,* or *psychological-psychosocial* in nature. The term psychological is used to denote sensorimotor capabilities that involve the child's knowledge of inanimate objects and his/her understanding of the relationships between objects. The attainments in the object permanence, means-ends abilities, and spatial relationships domains are primarily psychological in nature. The term psychosocial is used to describe sensorimotor capabilities involving knowledge of animate objects (i.e., other persons) and the child's understanding of relationships that exist between him/herself and other persons. The attainments of the vocal imitation, gestural imitation, and operational causality scales are primarily psychosocial behaviors. As is implied in the psychological-psychosocial term, this refers to the child's knowledge of both animate and inanimate objects. The Stage IV, V, and VI attainments of the scheme scale index primarily this type of sensorimotor capability.

The reason that it is useful to think of the sensorimotor attainments of Stage IV and V as being either psychological or psychosocial in nature, or a combination of both, is best understood when considered in terms of actual intervention activities. For example, if it were decided that the Stage IV coordination of behavioral acts in serialized and/or goal-directed sequences were to be taught, the following behaviors might be among those targeted as intervention objectives: looking around a barrier to see a puppet disappearing behind it, getting from a sitting to crawling position to obtain an out-of-reach object, reciprocal imitation between the child and adult of familiar vocal-gestural behaviors, extending the arms out to be picked up, turning a mirror around to view the reflection of both oneself and the parent sitting behind the child, and the child and adult taking turns using a spoon (a tool) to "feed" each other. Closer examination of the first, second, and third pairs of activities shows them to be, respectively, psychological, psychosocial, and psychological-psychosocial in nature. Viewing intervention activities in this manner helps one to remain cognizant of the multifaceted aspects of sensorimotor development, and helps to ensure that both psychologically oriented and psychosocially oriented cognitive capabilities are facilitated.

In actually implementing activities within Phase II, it is recommended that: 1) a wide variety of both psychological and psychosocial behaviors be facilitated in both Stages IV and V; 2) whenever possible, the activities should be designed to foster integrated psychological-psychosocial behaviors (e.g., playing a game of having the child open an adult's hand to remove a small toy seen hidden—integrated object permanence—operational causality); and 3) the activities be implemented within the naturalistic, ongoing context of the child's encounters with objects and persons. For example, in developing object permanence and related sensorimotor skills, rather than simply teaching the child to remove barriers to obtain objects hidden under them, the child should be taught to remove his/her clothes from a drawer, be taught where cereal, milk, spoons, and so on are kept, be taught to remove his/her toys from a toy box by lifting the lid of the container, and other such tasks. Again, this ensures that the behaviors facilitated become functional and adaptive.

Among the case studies presented above, Cases B, C, D, E, G, H, J, and K would have, as part of the intervention packages developed for them, activities designed to foster Phase II behaviors. An example of some of the principles involved in developing intervention packages from assessment results are described for Case E above.

Phase III

The major objective of the Phase III intervention procedures is to utilize *already manifested* behaviors to develop Stage VI–level cognitive-linguistic abilities. The overall goal of Phase III is to develop both symbolic-representational cognitive abilities and functional (semantic-communicative) language abilities.

The intervention activities in this final phase have been subdivided into three major categories: *cognition, semantics,* and *communication.* The cognitive activity sequences are specifically designed to foster two types of behaviors: representational problem solving and symbolic play. The activities designed to foster semantic language abilities have been further divided into five subcategories: prepositions, body parts, receptive language, direction following, and expressive language. The communication sequences are designed to foster both nonverbal and vocal communicative acts.

The objectives of the *representational problem solving* activity sequences of Phase III are to facilitate the child's abilities to infer the correct solution to problems from among various options and to use foresight in actually solving problem situations. For example, if the child had been taught to drop small balls through a funnel-type device to facilitate the "exploration of dropped objects" (a Phase II activity), he or she might now be given a number of different-size balls, several of which will not pass through the neck of the funnel. The objective of the activity would be to facilitate the ability to ignore attempting to place the larger balls into the funnel. Initially, the size of the large balls would be big enough so that discrimination is quite easy; the size of the balls should be gradually reduced so that finer discrimination is required to ignore the inappropriate-size balls.

The major objective of the *symbolic play* activity sequence of Phase III is to foster the ability to understand that one object can be used as a substitute for another in the absence of a functionally appropriate object. To accomplish this, activities are developed that require the child to successively abstract the salient features of objects that make them a substitute for another object. For example, if the child were being taught the salient/functional features of a spoon, he or she might be given a bowl of pudding and be taught that an adult-size spoon, child-size spoon, doll-size spoon, plastic spoon, wooden spoon, a flat spoon-shaped stick, and finally a tongue depressor can all be used to eat the pudding. The objective of this activity would be to get the child to recognize the tongue depressor as a substitute of a real spoon—thus facilitating the ability to recognize the salient/functional aspects of a spoon.

The objective of the *prepositional* language activity sequences is to foster the ability to understand such concepts as on, in, under, and behind. The ability to understand prepositions is taught by first having the child enact the behaviors himself or herself (e.g., getting into a box), and then having the child place objects in spatial configurations (e.g., putting toys into a box). The objective of the *body parts* activity sequences is to facilitate recognition of not only the parts of the body, but more importantly the relationship between body parts and specific actions that the particular parts are capable of performing. For example, if the child was being taught the body

part of hands, several actions associated with the movement of the hands (e.g., clapping, waving, washing) would be identified and the child would be taught the body part in the context of these actions (clap your hands, wave your hands, and wash your hands). To the maximum extent possible, all body parts are taught in this manner.

The major objective of the *receptive language* activity sequence of Phase III is to facilitate the ability to understand language that expresses the semantic constructions that comprise the contents that are learned during the child's initial acquisition of language (see Brown, 1973). All receptive language activities are taught within the context of functional learning situations. For example, if the child were being taught the word "cup," he or she would be shown a pitcher of juice, told "I have some juice for you," and told "get your cup" (which would be placed on the table next to the child within reach). At first only the cup would be placed on the table next to the child; gradually, irrelevant competing stimuli (e.g., a ball) and then functionally related objects (e.g., a spoon) would be introduced to foster the ability to obtain the cup within the context of several available objects.

The objective of the *direction following* activity sequences is to facilitate the ability to follow up to three component commands where the child is required to move from one location to another (which distinguishes the direction following from the receptive language training sequences). For example, an extension of the activity sequence just described for teaching the word "cup" might require the child to go to a cabinet to get a cup when told "I have some juice for you. Go get a cup and come back to the table." A standard back-chaining procedure is used to facilitate direction-following skills.

There are two objectives of the Phase III *expressive language* activity sequence. The first is to teach the child to imitate single and two-word utterances that describe objects, persons, and events in the context in which they are ordinarily encountered. The second objective is to foster the ability to name objects, persons, events, and actions, in response to "What's this?" and similar questions. For example, the child might be taught to imitate saying "baby" in the context of kissing or rocking a doll. Subsequently, the child might be asked to name the doll when asked "Who is this?" when the doll is taken out of a toy box. Generally, a shaping procedure is used to facilitate these stimulus-controlled language skills among children who do not spontaneously imitate and/or name objects, persons, and so on.

The objectives of the *communicative* activity sequences are to facilitate 1) the use of nonverbal gestures as communicative acts, 2) the concomitant use of nonverbal-vocal communicative behaviors (e.g., extending the arms out to be picked up in conjunction with a vocalization), and 3) the use of words (e.g., "more juice") as communicative behaviors for requests, demands, and so forth. Communicative acts are taught within the context of the natural occurrence of such behaviors. For example, if the child particularly liked to play with a ball, the object might be placed on a shelf out of the child's reach to facilitate pointing as a communicative act. Subsequently, the communicative partner may defer getting the ball, acting as if he or she doesn't understand what the child wants. Quite often, this elicits repeated pointing with a vocal accompaniment. Finally, the adult might say, following the child's use of pointing gesture, "Do you want the top or the ball?" as a means to elicit verbal communication.

The basic premise of the linguistic portion of the intervention procedures is that both the semantic and communicative aspects of language have sensorimotor antecedents that serve as the edifice in which linguistic behaviors are embedded (see Leonard, 1976). Furthermore, each aspect of language is considered to have sensorimotor precursors that are quite different in their nature and function. For example, Bates (1976) has proposed that the precursors for the communicative aspects of language are primarily *psychosocial* in nature, whereas Edmonds (1976) and Edwards (1973), among others, have contended that the precursors for the semantic aspects of language are primarily *psychological* in nature (see also Leonard, 1976; and Moerk, 1977).

Several lines of evidence have shown that Stage V performance in object permanence is significantly related to the onset of single words (e.g., Edmonds, 1976), whereas the use of vocalizations to *intentionally* communicate is significantly related to Stage V performance in psychosocial causality (Harding & Golinkoff, 1979). Moreover, it has been found that, once children begin speaking, semantic constructions are generally limited to actions that the children themselves perform (Edmonds, 1976). In other words, the linguistic abilities of children appear to be constrained by their sensorimotor capa-

bilities (see Edwards, 1973). Interestingly, the majority of agent-action-object propositions that constitute a large part of the child's first linguistic utterances describe the types of actions that are indexed by the scheme scale steps E_{51} and 8. Some evidence indicates that the ability to behaviorally enact such actions (incidently Stage V attainments) may be a prerequisite for the ability to understand and express such functional relationships (Bricker & Bricker, 1974). In a number of investigations of the language abilities of retarded and organically impaired children, it has been found that only children who have attained Stage V–VI functioning with regard to *both* the psychological and psychosocial aspects of sensorimotor development manifest functional language abilities (Dunst, 1978b). As can be seen, the distinction made earlier between knowledge of animate (psychosocial) and inanimate (psychological) objects was not made simply for heuristic purposes, but rather reflects existing knowledge concerning the acquisition of linguistic competence.

The somewhat complicated nature of this final phase of intervention can be reduced to a single issue—the nature of representational thought. According to Piaget (1973), the distinction between pre-Stage VI and Stage VI functioning is the ability to differentiate between *signifiers* and the *signified*. Signifiers (words, images, mental processes) are used to symbolize an object, person, or event in the *absence* of the actual thing that is signified. For example, in the area of representational problem solving, the child is considered to have used a symbolic function if it can be inferred that he/she has mentally enacted the problem-solving sequence prior to actually solving the problem (Berlyne, 1965, 1970). In the area of symbolic play, the child is considered to have used a signifier if he/she is capable of enacting a particular event without having the ordinarily used objects present.

Piaget (1973) also considers words to be signifiers when used in the absence of "reference-giving cues" (Flavell, 1963) for the persons, objects, or events they describe. For example, the use of the semantic construction "baby eat" to describe an event previously experienced or observed would indicate the child's ability to use the linguistic utterance as a signifier for that event. Likewise, the child's use of "more juice" as a communicative act in the absence of any cues (e.g., the child's cup) would indicate the child's ability to use the utterance as a signifier for request.

The activities in this final phase attempt to bridge the transition from prerepresentational to representational cognitive-linguistic abilities. *In every instance,* already manifested behaviors are modified in some manner to elicit the beginnings of symbolic processes. For example, in the development of symbolic play, hand movements might be used to have a child enact a series of behavioral actions that the child already has in his/her behavioral repertoire (e.g., pretending to pour water using the hand as a "cup").

The same procedure is used in developing language abilities. For example, if the child were able both to behaviorally enact "feeding a doll" and to understand the receptive command "get the cup," facilitating the ability to understand the more abstract command "give the baby a drink" would be taught by following this receptive "decoding" statement with "get the cup" and the modeling of the action of giving a drink to the doll. In this instance, the "give the baby a drink" statement would serve as the discriminative cue for the subsequent verbal and behavioral acts, where the word "drink" would eventually come to be understood in a symbolic manner.

In implementing activities in Phase III, it is recommended that two interrelated considerations always be addressed. First, behaviors to be taught should be extensions of *already* existing behavioral abilities. In other words, use what the child already "knows" to facilitate more advanced behaviors. Second, in implementing such a strategy, either modify or change the conditions or situations under which the child is to perform a given behavior, or add to an existing behavioral skill or set of skills a new behavior that will enhance the attainment of a more advanced cognitive-linguistic ability. The latter is exemplified in the receptive language training strategy briefly mentioned above. The former occurs when an attempt is made to "force" the child to attend to "something different" and *think* about the situation. For example, if a child had been taught to pick up a cup when presented with a pitcher of juice and told "get your cup," a situation might be contrived where the same is done and said, but with the cup replaced by a spoon. Experience has found that this type of problem situation tends to elicit "surprise" behaviors from the child, and thus forces the child to focus on the discrepant nature of the situation. Once this has occurred, the teacher can focus the child's attention on what is needed, and guide the child toward reducing the discrepancy (e.g., showing the child where the cups are kept). From a Piagetian perspective of development, such discrepancies (or optimal incongruence, in Hunt's (1961) terminology) are essential in the transition from lower to higher stages of functioning. An emphasis of intervention should therefore be to provide the child with the opportunity to resolve discrepant problem-solving situations.

Developing Intervention Packages

As had been suggested in several earlier sections of this manual, the development of intervention packages is recommended as the intervention procedure to be used to facilitate early cognitive-linguistic growth. Moreover, it was emphasized that the implementation of intervention packages be accomplished within the context where the behaviors would ordinarily be used and manifested. This ensures that the behaviors taught become functional and adaptive.

The intervention package approach is recommended for two reasons. First, such a strategy optimizes the efficacy of the intervention procedures. You can often get two or three times the return from a single effort. Second, this approach emphasizes, and therefore includes as part of its design, the synthesis, integration, and generalization of sensorimotor skills. This assures that an explicit effort is made to teach the child the interrelatedness of the achievements comprising the content of the sensorimotor period. In the design and implementation of intervention packages, the interventionist will most likely find that the child's transition from stage to stage is generally a less tedious process than he or she has most likely found to be the case with some children. Moreover, the interventionist should find that the learning process is a more enjoyable experience for not only the child, but the teacher as well.

REFERENCES

Bates, E. *Language and context: The acquisition of pragmatics.* New York: Academic Press, 1976.

Bayley, N. *The Bayley scales of infant development.* New York: The Psychological Corporation, 1969.

Berlyne, D. E. *Structure and direction in thinking.* New York: Wiley, 1965.

Berlyne, D. E. Children's reasoning and thinking. In P. Mussen (Ed.), *Carmichael's manual of child psychology* (Vol. 1), 3rd edition. New York: Wiley, 1970.

Best, B., & Roberts, G. Early cognitive development in hearing impaired children. *American Annals of the Deaf,* 1976, *121,* 560–564.

Bower, T. G. *Development in infancy.* San Francisco: Freeman, 1974.

Bricker, W., & Bricker, D. An early language training strategy. In R. Schiefelbusch & L. Lloyd (Eds.), *Language perspectives—Acquisitions, retardation, and intervention.* Baltimore: University Park Press, 1974.

Brown, R. *A first language: The early stages.* Cambridge, Mass.: Harvard University Press, 1973.

Campbell, S. Facilitation of cognitive and motor development in infants with central nervous system dysfunction. *Physical Therapy,* 1974, *54,* 346–353.

Casati, I., & Lezine, I. *Les étapes de l'intelligence sensorimotrice.* Paris: Editions du Centre de Psychologie Appliquée, 1968.

Cattell, P. *The measurement of intelligence of infants and young children.* New York: The Psychological Corporation, 1940.

Corman, H., & Escalona, S. Stages of sensorimotor development: A replication study. *Merrill-Palmer Quarterly,* 1969, *15,* 351–361.

Decarie, T. G. A study of the mental and emotional development of the thalidomide child. In B. Foss (Ed.), *Determinants of infant behavior* (Vol. 4). London: Methuen, 1969.

Didoha, J., & Dunst, C. J. Facilitating the acquisition of contingency awareness. In C. J. Dunst (Ed.), *Trends in early intervention services—Methods, models, and evaluation.* Arlington, Virginia: Department of Human Resources, 1975.

Dunst, C. J. The Northern Virginia Parent-Infant Education Program. In C. J. Dunst (Ed.), *Trends in early intervention services—Methods, models, and evaluation.* Arlington, Virginia: Department of Human Resources, 1975.

Dunst, C. J. The structure of infant intelligence: An historical overview. *Intelligence,* 1978, *2,* 321–331. (a)

Dunst, C. J. *The organization of sensorimotor intelligence among organically impaired children: Relationship to language acquisition and language retardation.* Unpublished paper, George Peabody College, Nashville, Tennessee, 1978. (b)

Dunst, C. J. A cognitive-social approach for assessment of early nonverbal communicative behavior. *Journal of Childhood Communication Disorders,* 1978, *2,* 110–123. (c)

Dunst, C. J. *An early cognitive-linguistic intervention strategy.* In preparation.

Dunst, C. J., & Brassell, W. R. The utility of Piaget's concept of decalage for the construction of cognitive based infant curricula. *North Carolina Journal of Mental Health,* 1975, *7,* 22–31.

Edmonds, M. New directions in theories of language acquisition. *Harvard Educational Review,* 1976, *46,* 175–198.

Edwards, D. Sensory-motor intelligence and semantic relations in early child grammar. *Cognition,* 1973, *2,* 395–434.

Escalona, S., & Corman, H. *The Albert Einstein scales of sensorimotor development.* Unpublished papers, Department of Psychiatry, Albert Einstein College of Medicine, New York, 1966.

Flavell, J. *The developmental psychology of Jean Piaget.* Princeton, N. J.: Van Nostrand, 1963.

Fraiberg, S. Parallel and divergent patterns in blind and sighted infants. *Psychoanalytic Study of the Child,* 1968, *23,* 264–300.

Fraiberg, S. The development of human attachments in infants blind from birth. *Merrill-Palmer Quarterly,* 1975, *21,* 315–334.

Green, B. A method of scalogram analysis using summary statistics. *Psychometrika,* 1956, *21,* 79–88.

Griffiths, R. *The abilities of babies.* London: University of London Press, 1954.

Guttman, L. The basis for scalogram analysis. In S. Stouffer (Ed.), *Measurement and prediction.* Princeton, N.J.: Princeton University Press, 1950.

Harding, C., & Golinkoff, R. The origins of intentional vocalizations in prelinguistic infants. *Child Development,* 1979, *50,* 33–40.

Hunt, J. McV. *Intelligence and experience.* New York: Ronald Press, 1961.

Hunt, J. McV. Piaget's observations as a source of hypotheses concerning motivation. *Merrill-Palmer Quarterly,* 1963, *9,* 263–275.

Hunt, J. McV. Toward a theory of guided learning in development. In R. Ojemann & K. Pritchett (Eds.), *Giving emphasis to guided learning.* Cleveland, Ohio: Educational Research Council, 1966.

Hunt, J. McV. Psychological assessment in education and social class. In R. Harth, E. Meyen, & G. Nelson (Eds.), *The legal and educational consequences of the intelligence testing movement.* Proceedings of the Missouri Conference on Special Education, University of Missouri-Columbia, 1972.

Hunt, J. McV. The utility of ordinal scales inspired by Piaget's observations. *Merrill-Palmer Quarterly,* 1976, *22,* 31–45.

Hunt, J. McV. *Specificity in early development and experience.* Lecture presented at the Meyer Children's Rehabilitation Institute, University of Nebraska Medical Center, Omaha, Nebraska, 1977. (a)

Hunt, J. McV. *Implications of plasticity and hierarchical achievements for the assessment of development and risk of mental retardation.* Paper presented at a symposium entitled "Psychological Risks During Pregnancy,

Birth, and Early Infancy: Assessment and Prediction," University of Texas, Austin, 1977. (b)

Hunt, J. McV. Psychological development: Early experiences. *Annual Review of Psychology*, 1979, *30*, 103–143.

Hunt, J. McV. *Experiential roots of intentions, initiative, and trust.* Paper written for a volume to honor the memory of Daniel Ellis Berlyne. In preparation.

Hunt, J. McV., Mohandessi, K., Ghodssi, M., & Akiyama, M. The psychological development of orphanage-reared infants: Interventions with outcomes. *Genetic Psychology Monographs*, 1976, *94*, 177–226.

Hunt, J. McV., Paraskevopoulos, J., Schickedanz, D., & Uzgiris, I. Variations in the mean age of achieving object permanence under diverse conditions of rearing. In B. Friedlander, G. Sterritt, & G. Kirk (Eds.), *The exceptional infant: Assessment and intervention* (Vol. 3). New York: Brunner/Mazel, 1975.

Kahn, J. Utility of the Uzgiris and Hunt scales of sensorimotor development with severely and profoundly retarded children. *American Journal of Mental Deficiency*, 1976, *80*, 663–665.

King, W., & Seegmiller, B. Performance of 14- to 22-month-old black, firstborn male infants on two tests of cognitive development. *Developmental Psychology*, 1973, *8*, 317–326.

Kopp, C., Sigman, M., & Parmelee, A. Ordinality and sensory-motor series. *Child Development*, 1973, *44*, 821–823.

Kopp, C., Sigman, M., & Parmelee, A. Longitudinal study of sensorimotor development. *Developmental Psychology*, 1974, *10*, 687–695.

Lewis, M., & McGurk, H. Infant intelligence. *Science*, 1972, *178*, 1174–1176.

Leonard, L. *Meaning in child language: Issues in the study of early semantic development.* New York: Grune and Stratton, 1976.

Lezak, M. *Neuropsychological assessment.* New York: Oxford University Press, 1976.

Lowe, M. Trends in the development of representational play in infants from one to three years. *Journal of Child Psychology and Psychiatry*, 1975, *16*, 33–47.

McCall, R., Hogarty, P., & Hurlburt, N. Transitions in infant sensorimotor development and the prediction of childhood IQ. *American Psychologist*, 1972, *27*, 728–748.

Miller, D., Cohen, L., & Hill, K. A methodological investigation of Piaget's theory of object concept development in the sensory-motor period. *Journal of Experimental Child Psychology*, 1970, *9*, 59–68.

Moerk, E. *Pragmatic and semantic aspects of early language development.* Baltimore: University Park Press, 1977.

Paraskevopoulos, J., & Hunt, J. McV. Object construction and imitation under differing conditions of rearing. *Journal of Genetic Psychology*, 1971, *119*, 301–321.

Piaget, J. *The origins of intelligence in children.* (M. Cook, trans.). New York: International Universities Press, 1936.

Piaget, J. *The construction of reality in the child.* (M. Cook, trans.). New York: Basic Books, 1937.

Piaget, J. *Play, dreams, and imitation in childhood.* (C. Gattegno & F. Hodgson, trans.). New York: Norton, 1945.

Piaget, J. The general problems of the psychobiological development of the child. In J. Tanner & B. Inhelder (Eds.), *Discussions on child development* (Vol. 4). New York: International Universities Press, 1960.

Piaget, J. *The child and reality: Problems of genetic psychology.* (A. Rosin, trans.). New York: Grossman, 1973.

Pinard, A., & Laurendeau, M. "Stage" in Piaget's cognitive-developmental theory: Exegesis of a concept. In D. Elkind & J. Flavell (Eds.), *Studies in cognitive development.* New York: Oxford University Press, 1969.

Robinson, C., Chatelanat, G., Spritzer, S., Robertson, M., & Bricker, W. Study of sensorimotor development in young developmentally delayed and nondelayed children. In D. Bricker & W. Bricker (Eds.), Infant, toddler, and preschool research and intervention project: Report—Year III, *IMRID Behavioral Science Monograph*, No. 23, Nashville, Tennessee: George Peabody College, 1973.

Rogers, S. Characteristics of the cognitive development of profoundly retarded children. *Child Development*, 1977, *48*, 837–843.

Silverstein, A., Brownlee, L., Hubbell, M., & McLain, R. Comparison of two sets of Piagetian scales with severely and profoundly retarded children. *American Journal of Mental Deficiency*, 1975, *80*, 292–297.

Spritzer, S. Assessment of means-ends behavior with delayed and nondelayed infants, toddlers, and preschool age children. In D. Bricker & W. Bricker (Eds.), Infant, toddler, and preschool research and intervention project: Report—Year III, *IMRID Behavioral Science Monograph*, No. 23. Nashville, Tennessee: George Peabody College, 1973.

Sugarman, S. Some organizational aspects of pre-verbal communication. In I. MarKova (Ed.), *The social context of language.* New York: Wiley, 1978.

Tessier, F. The development of young cerebral palsied children according to Piaget's sensorimotor theory. *Dissertation Abstracts International*, 1969/70, *30A*, 4841.

Uzgiris, I. Ordinality in the development of schemes for relating to objects. In J. Hellmuth (Ed.), *The exceptional infant: The normal infant* (Vol. 1). New York: Brunner/Mazel, 1967.

Uzgiris, I. Patterns of vocal and gestural imitation in infants. In F. Monks, W. Hartrup, & J. deWit (Eds.), *Determinants of development.* New York: Academic Press, 1972.

Uzgiris, I. Patterns of cognitive development in infancy. *Merrill-Palmer Quarterly*, 1973, *19*, 181–204.

Uzgiris, I. Organization of sensorimotor intelligence. In M. Lewis (Ed.), *Origins of intelligence: Infancy and early childhood.* New York: Plenum Press, 1976. (a)

Uzgiris, I. Infant development from a Piagetian approach: Introduction to a symposium. *Merrill-Palmer Quarterly*, 1976, *22*, 3–10. (b)

Uzgiris, I. Some observations on early cognitive development. In M. Appel & L. Goldberg (Eds.), *Topics in cognitive development* (Vol. 1). New York: Plenum, 1977. (a)

Uzgiris, I. Commentary and reply: Transitions in early mental development. *Monograph of the Society for Research in Child Development,* 1977, *42,* no. 3 (Serial No. 171). (b)

Uzgiris, I., & Hunt, J. McV. *Assessment in infancy: Ordinal scales of psychological development.* Urbana: University of Illinois Press, 1975.

Watson, J. S. The development and generalization of "contingency awareness" in early infancy: Some hypotheses. *Merrill-Palmer Quarterly,* 1966, *12,* 123–136.

White, B. *Human infants: Experience and psychological development.* Englewood Cliffs, N.J.: Prentice Hall, 1971.

Woodward, M. The behavior of idiots interpreted by Piaget's theory of sensorimotor development. *British Journal of Educational Psychology,* 1959, *29,* 60–71.

APPENDICES

APPENDICES

SUMMARY RECORD FORM
PROFILE OF ABILITIES FORM
INDIVIDUAL SCALE RECORD FORMS

Uzgiris and Hunt Scales of Infant Psychological Development
SUMMARY RECORD FORM

Name _____ Sex _____

Date of birth _____ Date of test _____

Examiner _____

Comments:

	Year	Month	Day
Date of test	_____	_____	_____
Date of birth	_____	_____	_____
Chronological age	_____	_____	_____
Chronological age (adjusted)			_____

Scale	Highest Developmental Attainment	Scale Step	Stage Placement	EDA	Deviation Score
Object Permanence					
Means-Ends					
Vocal Imitation					
Gestural Imitation					
Causality					
Space					
Schemes					

SUMMARY SCORES

Stage Placements

Mode	Range

EDAs

Average	Range

Deviation Scores

Average	Range

QUALITATIVE CHARACTERISTICS OF SENSORIMOTOR DEVELOPMENT

Uzgiris and Hunt Scales of Infant Psychological Development
PROFILE OF ABILITIES FORM

Child's Name _____
Date of Birth _____
Examiner _____
Comments: _____

Sex _____
Age _____
Date of Test _____

STAGES OF DEVELOPMENT

	Object Permanence	Means-Ends Abilities	Vocal Imitation	Gestural Imitation	Operational Causality	Spatial Relationships	Scheme Actions
VI	14 E_7 13 12 11 10	E_{19} E_{18} 13 E_{17} 12	9	9	7	11b E_{47}	E_{53} 10
V	9 8 E_6 7 6	E_{14}, E_{15}, E_{16} 11 E_{13} 10 E_{12} 9 E_{11} 8	E_{25} 8	E_{33} E_{31}, E_{32} 8 E_{30} E_{28}, E_{29} 7	6 E_{37} 5 E_{36} E_{35}	11a 10 E_{46} 9 8 E_{45}	9 E_{52} 8
IV	E_5 5 E_4 E_3	7 6 E_{10} 5	7b 7a 6 5b 5a	6 5 4b 4a	4c 4b 4a	E_{43}, E_{44} E_{41}, E_{42} 7 E_{39}, E_{40} 6	E_{51} 7 6
III	4 3 E_2	E_9 4 3 2	E_{23} 4c 4b 4a E_{22}	3 2 E_{27}	3c, 3d 3a, 3b 2	5 4	5 E_{50} 4 3
II	2 1	1	E_{21} 3 2b 2a 1	1b 1a	1	3 2 1	2 1 E_{49}
I	E_1	E_8	E_{20}	E_{26}	E_{34}	E_{38}	E_{48}

SENSORIMOTOR DOMAINS

I: VISUAL PURSUIT AND THE PERMANENCE OF OBJECTS   Child's Name _____ Date of Birth _____ Date of Test _____

SCALE STEP	AGE PLACEMENT (Months)	DEVELOP-MENTAL STAGE	ELICITING CONTEXT	CRITICAL ACTION CODE	CRITICAL BEHAVIORS	SCORING					OBSERVATIONS
						1	2	3	4	5	
E₁	1	I	Visual Fixation	—	Fixates on object held 8 to 10 inches above the eyes						
1	2	II	Visual Tracking	1d	Tracks object through a 180° arc						
2	3	II	Visual Tracking	2c	Lingers at point of object's disappearance—child in supine position or in an infant seat						
E₂	4	III	Visual Tracking	—	Searches for object at point of disappearance—child seated on parent's lap						
3	5	III	Visible Displacement	3c	Secures partially hidden object						
4	6	III	Visual Tracking	2d	Returns glance to position above the head after object moves out of visual field						
E₃	7	IV	Visual Tracking	—	Reverses searching for object in anticipation of reappearance—child seated on parent's lap						
E₄	7	IV	Visible Displacement	—	Withdraws object held in hand following covering of hand and object with cloth						
5	8	IV	Visible Displacement	4d	Secures object hidden under a single screen						
E₅	9	IV	Visible Displacement	5b	Secures object hidden with two screens (A & B)—hidden under A twice then B—searches under A only						
6	9	V	Visible Displacement	6c	Secures object hidden under one of two screens—hidden alternately						
7	9	V	Visible Displacement	7c	Secures object hidden under one of three screens—hidden alternately						
E₆	10	V	Successive Visible Displacement	8e	Secures object hidden through a series of successive visible displacements with three screens						
8	10	V	Superimposed Screens	9c	Secures object under three superimposed screens						
9	13	V	Invisible Displacement	10d 10e	Secures object hidden with a single screen						
10	14	VI	Invisible Displacement	11c	Secures object hidden with two screens (A & B)—hidden under A twice then B						
11	14	VI	Invisible Displacement	12c	Secures object hidden under one of two screens—hidden alternately						
12	15	VI	Invisible Displacement	13c	Secures object hidden under one of three screens—hidden alternately						
13	18	VI	Successive Invisible Displacement	14c	Secures object hidden with three screens—object left under last screen—child searches along pathway						
E₇	22	VI	Successive Invisible Displacement	14d	Secures object hidden with three screens—object left under last screen—child searches directly under last screen						
14	23	VI	Successive Invisible Displacement	15c	Secures object hidden with three screens—object left under first screen—child searches in reverse order						

II: DEVELOPMENT OF MEANS FOR OBTAINING DESIRED ENVIRONMENTAL EVENTS

Child's Name_____ Date of Birth_____ Date of Test_____

SCALE STEP	AGE PLACEMENT (Months)	DEVELOP-MENTAL STAGE	ELICITING CONTEXT	CRITICAL ACTION CODE	CRITICAL BEHAVIORS	SCORING 1	2	3	4	5	OBSERVATIONS
E_8	2	I	Visual Awareness	—	Activity level increases or decreases on seeing a visually presented object						
1	2	II	Hand Watching	1b	Child engages in hand watching						
2	3	III	Secondary Circular Reaction	3c	Repeats arm movements to keep a toy activated						
3	4	III	Visually Directed Reaching	2b	Visually directed reaching—hand and object both in view						
4	5	III	Visual Directed Reaching	2c	Visually directed reaching—brings closed hand up to object						
E_9	5	III	Visually Directed Reaching	2d	Visually directed reaching—shapes hand in anticipation of securing object						
5	7	IV	Multiple Objects	4c	Drops one or both objects held in hands to obtain a third object						
E_{10}	8	IV	Barrier	—	Pushes obstruction (e.g., pillow or Plexiglas) out of the way to obtain an object						
6	8	IV	Support	6d 6c	Pulls support to obtain an object placed on it						
7	9	IV	Locomotion	5c	Uses some form of locomotion as a means to obtain an out-of-reach object						
8	10	V	Support	7c	Does not pull support with object held above it						
E_{11}	10	V	Support	—	Does not pull either of two supports with object placed between them						
9	11	V	String (horizontal)	8c 8d	Pulls string along a horizontal surface to obtain an object attached to it						
E_{12}	12	V	String (horizontal)	—	Pulls the correct one of two strings to obtain an object attached to one string						
10	13	V	String (vertical)	9e 9f	Uses string vertically—pulls object up from floor						
E_{13}	18	V	T-Stick	—	Uses T-stick as a tool to obtain an out-of-reach object						
11	19	V	Stick	10d 10e	Uses a stick as a tool to obtain an out-of-reach object						
E_{14}	19	V	Matchbox	—	Opens and removes the contents of a small matchbox						
E_{15}	19	V	Necklace (container)	11d	Invents method to place the necklace into the container						
E_{16}	19	V	Solid Ring	12c	Solid ring—attempts to stack avoids subsequently						
12	20	VI	Necklace (container)	11e	Shows foresight in placing the necklace into the container						
E_{17}	20	VI	Matchbox		Shows foresight in placing a chain into a matchbox						
13	24	VI	Solid Ring	12d	Shows foresight by not stacking the solid ring						
E_{18}	24	VI	Tube (clear)		Uses stick to push out a toy inserted in a clear tube						
E_{19}	26	VI	Tube (opaque)		Uses stick to push out a toy inserted in an opaque tube						

IIIA: DEVELOPMENT OF VOCAL IMITATION

Child's Name _____ Date of Birth _____ Date of Test _____

SCALE STEP	AGE PLACEMENT (Months)	DEVELOP-MENTAL STAGE	ELICITING CONTEXT	CRITICAL ACTION CODE	CRITICAL BEHAVIORS	SCORING 1	2	3	4	5	OBSERVATIONS
E$_{20}$	1	I	Vocal Responsiveness	—	Responds to voice						
1	1	II	Spontaneous Vocalizations	1b	Vocalizes other than crying						Observed ___ ___ ___ ___ ___ Reported ___ ___ ___ ___ ___
2a	2	II	Cooing Sounds	2c	Shows positive response to familiar cooing sounds						Presented / Positive Response / Vocalizes / Imitates
2b	3	II	Babbling Sounds	3c	Shows positive response to familiar babbling sounds						Presented / Positive Response / Vocalizes / Imitates
3	3	II	Cooing Sounds	2d	Vocalizes in response to cooing sounds						
E$_{21}$	3	II	Cooing Sounds	2e	Vocalizes similar sounds in response to cooing sounds						
E$_{22}$	3	III	Cooing Sounds	2f	Imitates cooing sounds						
4a	4	III	Babbling Sounds	3d	Vocalizes in response to babbling sounds						
4b	6	III	Babbling Sounds	3e	Vocalizes similar sounds in response to babbling sounds						
4c	9	III	Words (familiar)	4b	Vocalizes in response to familiar words						Presented / Positive Response / Vocalizes / Imitates
E$_{23}$	9	III	Words (familiar)	—	Vocalizes similar sounds in response to familiar words						
5a	12	IV	Babbling Sounds	3f	Imitates babbling sounds						
5b	12	IV	Words (familiar)	4c	Imitates familiar words						
6	12	IV	Unfamiliar Sound Patterns	5d	Vocalizes in response to unfamiliar sound patterns (examples: room-room, ree-ree, ding-dong, brr, ssss, zzz)						Presented / Vocalizes / Imitates GA / Imitates
7a	14	IV	Unfamiliar Sound Patterns	5e	Imitates unfamiliar sound patterns by gradual approximation (GA)						

Child's Name_____ Date of Birth_____ Date of Test_____

SCALE STEP	AGE PLACEMENT (Months)	DEVELOP-MENTAL STAGE	ELICITING CONTEXT	CRITICAL ACTION CODE	CRITICAL BEHAVIORS	SCORING					OBSERVATIONS
						1	2	3	4	5	
7b	15	IV	Novel Words	6c	Imitates novel words by gradual approximation (GA) (examples: pretty, bounce, uppity, bottle, bus, flower, bunny, fish, beads)						Presented Vocalizes ImitatesGA Imitates _____ _____ _____ _____ _____ _____ _____ _____ _____ _____ _____ _____ _____ _____ _____ _____
8	17	V	Unfamiliar Sound Patterns	5f	Imitates unfamiliar sound patterns						
E24	18	V	Novel Words	—	Imitates one novel word						
E25	20	V	Novel Words	6d	Imitates two novel words						
9	23	VI	Novel Words	6e	Imitates at least four novel words						

Child's Name_____Date of Birth_____Date of Test_____

SCALE STEP	AGE PLACEMENT (Months)	DEVELOP- MENTAL STAGE	ELICITING CONTEXT	CRITICAL ACTION CODE	CRITICAL BEHAVIORS	SCORING					OBSERVATIONS			
						1	2	3	4	5				
E₂₆	2	I	Visual Attention	—	Attends to gestures performed by an adult									
1a	6	II	Simple Gestures	1b	Performs consistent act in response to familiar, simple gestures (examples: patting table, squeezing a toy, shaking a rattle, banging a table with a spoon)						Presented	Positive Response	Imitates GA	Imitates
1b	7	II	Complex Gestures	2b	Performs consistent act in response to complex gestures composed of familiar schemes (examples: crumples paper, slides beads, pat-a-cake, hitting blocks together, opening and closing a Slinky)						Presented	Positive Response	Imitates GA	Imitates
E₂₇	8	III	Simple Gestures	—	Imitates familiar, simple gestures by gradual approximation (GA)									
2	8	III	Simple Gestures	1c	Imitates simple, familiar gestures									
3	8	III	Complex Gestures	2c	Attempts to imitate complex gestures composed of familiar schemes									
4a	9	IV	Complex Gestures	2d	Imitates complex gestures composed of familiar schemes by gradual approximation (GA)									
4b	11	IV	Visible Gestures (unfamiliar)	3c	Imitates unfamiliar, visible gestures by gradual approximation (GA) (examples: snapping fingers, bending index finger, playing "so-big," using the hand as a puppet)						Presented	Positive Response	Imitates GA	Imitates
5	12	IV	Complex Gestures	2e	Imitates complex gestures composed of familiar schemes									
6	15	IV	Visible Gestures (unfamiliar)	3d	Imitates unfamiliar, visible gestures									
7	18	V	Invisible Gestures	4b	Attempts to imitate unfamiliar, invisible gestures (examples: hat on head, tap head, wrinkle nose, put beads behind the neck, hands over ears, pull earlobe)						Presented	Positive Response	Imitates GA	Imitates
E₂₈	18	V	Invisible Gesture (object)	4c	Imitates invisible gesture with object by gradual approximation (GA)									
E₂₉	18	V	Invisible Gesture	4c	Imitates invisible gesture without object by gradual approximation (GA)									
E₃₀	19	V	Invisible Gesture (object)	4d	Imitates one invisible gesture with object									
8	20	V	Invisible Gesture	4d	Imitates one invisible gesture without object									

SCALE STEP	AGE PLACEMENT (Months)	DEVELOP- MENTAL STAGE	ELICITING CONTEXT	CRITICAL ACTION CODE	CRITICAL BEHAVIORS	SCORING					OBSERVATIONS
						1	2	3	4	5	
E$_{31}$	20	V	Invisible Gestures (object)		Imitates two invisible gestures with object						
E$_{32}$	20	V	Invisible Gestures		Imitates two invisible gestures without object						
E$_{33}$	22	V	Invisible Gestures (object)	4e	Imitates three invisible gestures with object						
9	23	VI	Invisible Gestures	4e	Imitates three invisible gestures without object						

IV: DEVELOPMENT OF OPERATIONAL CAUSALITY   Child's Name_____ Date of Birth_____ Date of Test_____

SCALE STEP	AGE PLACEMENT (Months)	DEVELOP-MENTAL STAGE	ELICITING CONTEXT	CRITICAL ACTION CODE	CRITICAL BEHAVIORS	SCORING 1	2	3	4	5	OBSERVATIONS
E_{34}	2	I	Social Responsiveness	—	Vocalizes and/or smiles in response to adult talking						
1	2	II	Hand Watching	1b	Engages in hand watching						
2	3	III	Secondary Circular Reaction	2c	Repeats arm movements to keep a toy activated						
3a	5	III	Response to Interesting Spectacle	3c	Uses procedure as causal action in response to adult producing a repetitive action with toy (jumping jack, pinwheel, any string-activated toy)						Action Presented _____ Procedure Used _____
3b	5	III	Familiar Game	4c	Uses procedure as causal action in familiar game situations (pulls-to-sit, pat-a-cake, tickling tummy)						Game ___ Procedure Used ___ Other Causal Action ___
3c	5	III	Spectacle Created by Agent	5c	Uses procedure as causal action in response to behavior created by an agent (no toy) (snapping fingers, mouth sound, "beeping" the nose)						Action Presented ___ Procedure Used ___ Other Causal Action ___
3d	5	III	Spectacle Created Using Toy	6b	Uses procedure as causal action in response to behavior created by an agent using a toy (Slinky, Farmer Says, whistling sound using a pop-bead)						Action Presented ___ Procedure Used ___ Other Causal Action ___
4a	10	IV	Spectacle Created by Agent	5d	Touches adult's hands as causal action behavior created by agent—no toy						
4b	10	IV	Spectacle Created Using Toy	6c	Touches adult's hands or object as causal action—behavior by agent—using a toy						
4c	10	IV	Spectacle Created by Toy	7c	Touches adult's hands or object as causal action in response to adult activating a mechanical toy						
E_{35}	12	V	Engages Adult	—	Pushes or pulls an adult's hands to have a behavior instigated or repeated						
E_{36}	12	V	Repeats Behavior	—	Repeats behavior (shows off) to maintain adult attention						Behaviors Used:
5	14	V	Engages Adult	6d 7d	Gives object to adult as causal action to have it activated						
E_{37}	15	V	Gestural-Vocal Causal Behavior	—	Uses gestural plus visual/vocal behaviors to have an adult repeat or instigate a desired action						Gestures Used ___ Vocalization ___
6	18	V	Spectacle Created by Toy	7e	Attempts to activate mechanical toy following demonstration						
7	21	VI	Spectacle Created by Toy	7f	Searches for causal mechanism needed to activate a wind-up toy (no demonstration)						

V: CONSTRUCTION OF OBJECTS IN SPACE   Child's Name_____ Date of Birth_____ Date of Test_____

SCALE STEP	AGE PLACEMENT (Months)	DEVELOP-MENTAL STAGE	ELICITING CONTEXT	CRITICAL ACTION CODE	CRITICAL BEHAVIORS	SCORING 1	2	3	4	5	OBSERVATIONS
E38	2	I	Visual Orientation	—	Searches for sound with eyes						
1	2	II	Visual Scanning	1b	Alternates glance slowly between two visually presented objects						
2	3	II	Visual Scanning	1c	Alternates glance rapidly between two visually presented objects						
3	4	II	Sound Localization	2d	Localizes the source of sound						
4	5	III	Visually Directed Reaching	3d	Secures visually presented objects						
5	6	III	Follows Trajectory	4c	Follows trajectory of objects falling within view						
6	7	IV	Follows Trajectory	4e	Follows trajectory of objects falling out of view						
E39	9	IV	Reverses Objects	5c	Turns mirror over to view functional side						
E40	9	IV	Reverses Objects	5c	Turns photograph or other picture around to view functional side						
7	9	IV	Reverses Objects	5c	Rotates three-dimensional objects to view functional side						
E41	10	IV	Combining Objects	6c	Places (drops) objects into a container						
E42	10	IV	Combining Objects	—	Stirs with a spoon in a cup						
E43	10	IV	Combining Objects	—	Uses hammer-stick to play xylophone						
E44	10	IV	Combining Objects	—	Bangs spoon on inverted cup						
E45	13	IV	Combining Objects	—	Dumps contents out of a narrow-necked container						
8	14	V	Combining Objects	6d	Places objects into a cup—dumps out contents						
9	14	V	Combining Objects	7c	Builds tower of two cubes						
E46	15	V	Combining Objects	—	Places rings on a stacking stick						
10	15	V	Combining Objects	8c	Allows an object to move down an incline						
11a	16	V	Detour (simple)	10c	Makes simple detour to obtain a desired object						
E47	18	VI	Detour (complex)	—	Makes complex detour from cul-de-sac to obtain a desired object						
11b	18	VI	Indicates Person's Absence	11c	Indicates the absence of familiar persons						

VI: DEVELOPMENT OF SCHEMES FOR RELATING TO OBJECTS

Child's Name_____ Date of Birth_____ Date of Test_____

SCALE STEP	AGE PLACEMENT (Months)	DEVELOP-MENTAL STAGE	ELICITING CONTEXT	CRITICAL ACTION CODE	CRITICAL BEHAVIORS	SCORING 1	2	3	4	5	OBSERVATIONS
E_{48}	1	I	Grasping Reaction	—	Grasps examiner's finger						
E_{49}	2	II	Retention of Objects	a	Retains object placed in hands for 10 to 15 seconds						
1	3	II	Mouthing	b	Mouths objects placed in the hand						
2	3	II	Visual Inspection	c	Visually inspects objects held in the hands						
3	5	III	Simple Schemes	d_1	Uses simple motor schemes (banging or hitting objects on a table surface)						
4	6	III	Simple Schemes	d_2	Uses simple motor schemes (shaking, waving, etc.) independent of hitting a surface						
E_{50}	7	III	Letting Go	—	Drops or throws objects—no visual monitoring of action						
5	7	III	Examining	e	Rotates objects, examining the various sides						
6	9	IV	Complex Actions	f	Uses complex motor schemes (slides, crumples, swings, tears, etc.)						
7	10	IV	Letting Go	g	Drops or throws objects—visual monitoring of results of action/terminal location of object						
E_{51}	11	IV	Social Actions	h	Socially instigated actions—self and/or others						Actions Observed:
8	13	V	Social Actions	h	Socially instigated actions—inanimate objects						Actions Observed:
E_{52}	14	V	Giving	—	Gives object to another person to instigate social interaction						Objects Used:
9	15	V	Showing	i	Shows objects (does not give) to others						Objects Used:
10	19	VI	Naming	j	Spontaneously names objects, persons, actions, etc.						Objects Persons Actions _____ _____ _____ _____ _____ _____ _____ _____ _____
E_{53}	24	VI	Symbolic Play	—	Symbolic play—uses one object as a signifier for another object (e.g., a stick for a spoon)						Signified Signifier _____ _____ _____ _____

appendix B

DESCRIPTIONS OF THE EXPERIMENTAL ASSESSMENT ITEMS

Each experimental assessment item specifies: 1) the position or location of the child, or the situation that needs to be arranged; 2) the object or objects needed to administer the item; 3) the directions and instructions for administering the item; and 4) the response (critical action) that indicates that the child has attained a particular level of functioning.

Assessment items that have directions that Uzgiris and Hunt (1975) describe in their monograph are not repeated in the descriptions presented here. Rather, the pages on which the directions are specified are referenced, and the examiner should refer to the Uzgiris and Hunt monograph for the administration instructions.

I: OBJECT PERMANENCE

E₁: **Fixates on object held 8 to 10 inches above the child's eyes.**

Location: The child may be supine on the floor or in a crib, in an infant seat, or held by the parent in a supine position.

Object: Any bright object that attracts the child's attention and that makes a sound when moved (e.g., a roly-poly).

Directions: Hold the object about 8 to 10 inches in front of the child's eyes. Shake the object gently to attract the child's attention. Repeat several times if necessary.

Response: Child fixates on the object momentarily either each time it is shaken or when the child's visual gaze moves across the object.

E₂: **Searches for object at point of disappearance.**

Location: The child may be seated on the parent's lap, in a high chair, in an infant seat positioned at least 45° toward the vertical, or sitting by him/herself on the floor.

Object: Any bright object attached to a string 18 to 24 inches long that attracts the child's attention, but *does not* make any sound when moved.

Directions: Stand behind the child and suspend the toy in front of him/her about 18 to 24 inches from his/her face. When the child focuses on the object, move it in a slow circular trajectory around the child so that it disappears and reappears on three occasions. On the fourth trajectory, move the object around the child to the side opposite the point of disappearance but slightly behind the child so as not to be visible. Repeat several times, varying the side to which the object is made to disappear.

Response: Child turns eyes, head, and/or body toward the side of the object's disappearance looking for the vanished object.

E₃: Reverses searching in anticipation of the reappearance of an object.

Location: Same as in E₂.

Object: Same as in E₂.

Directions: Same as in E₂.

Response: Child turns in direction of trajectory but, failing to find the object, reverses his/her searching to the opposite side to find and/or anticipate the reappearance of the object; or, child turns directly to the opposite side once the object moves out of the visual field in anticipation of the reappearance of the object.

E₄: Withdraws object being played with following covering of the object and the child's hand.

Location: The child may be seated in a high chair, on the parent's lap at a table, at a small table by him/herself, or on the floor by him/herself. It is important that the child have both hands free to manipulate the test materials, and be seated at a surface large enough to accommodate the test materials. For children who do not yet sit independently and/or do not have control of their upper torsos, it is important to have the child held or propped so as to minimize these motoric variables as factors in the assessment.

Object: Any object or toy that the child demonstrates interest in, and that he/she enjoys playing with. An opaque screen (cloth) about 18 inches × 18 inches.

Directions: While the child is holding the object and is both actively playing with it (e.g., banging it) and visually monitoring the play activity, place a screen over *both* the object and the child's hand, making both invisible.

Response: Child withdraws the object from beneath the screen, or removes the screen impeding visual contact with the free hand.

E₅: Secures object hidden under one of two screens.

Location: Same as in E₄.

Object: Same as in E₄ and a second opaque screen.

Directions: Following the child's successful retrieval of an object hidden under a single screen (scale step 5), place a second screen next to the first one. Hide a toy under the first screen (A) several more times. Then, switch the hiding location to the second screen (B).

Response: Child searches for the object hidden under screen A on all three occasions, even following the object's displacement under screen B.

Note: If the child secures the object when hidden under screen B, this hiding counts as the first presentation for scale step 6. Searching for the object under A following its displacement under B is termed the "Stage IV pattern error," and scale step E_5 was added to the assessment pool because this response is often observed when an object is hidden under a second screen, even though the child has watched where the object was hidden.

E_6: **Secures an object hidden through a series of successive visible displacements.**

Location: Same as in E_4.

Object: Any object of interest to the child and three opaque screens.

Directions: See Uzgiris and Hunt, pp. 158–159.

Response: Child searches directly under the last screen in the path.

E_7: **Secures an object following a series of successive invisible displacements with three screens.**

Location: Same as in E_4.

Object: Any object of interest to the child and three opaque screens.

Directions: See Uzgiris and Hunt, pp. 162–163.

Response: Child searches directly under the last screen in the pathway rather than in the order of hiding.

Note: E_7 is considered a possible intervening scale step only if scale step 14 is not attained. Moreover, the E_7 response is necessary for presentation of the scale step 14 item (see Uzgiris & Hunt, p. 163).

II: MEANS-ENDS ABILITIES

E_8: **Activity level shifts on visual presentation of an object.**

Location: The child may be supine on the floor or in a crib, or in an infant seat.

Object: Any bright object that attracts the child's attention, but that makes no sound when moved. Both the child's arms and legs should be free to move during the presentation of this item.

Directions: The item presentation should be initiated when the child's arms are resting on the floor or crib surface, or next to the child's sides if in an infant seat. The object is held about 18 inches from the child's face and is slowly brought into the child's line of vision. As soon as the child focuses on the object, it is moved quickly to within six inches of the child's face, where it is held for about 10 seconds. The object should be presented to the midline and to both the child's left and right sides (about 45° from the midline).

Response: Following the sudden presentation of the object, the child's activity level shifts; increases if quiet and still, decreases if moderately active. The child must show that he/she recognizes the change of position of the object (i.e., visually adapts to the changes in the stimulus distance).

E₈: **Secures visually presented object by opening the hand in anticipation of grasping the object.**

Location: Same as in E₈, or seated by him/herself on the floor.

Object: Any object of interest to the child, but one with some part of the object small enough to be easily grasped.

Directions: See Uzgiris and Hunt, pp. 165–166.

Response: While reaching for the object, the hand opens in anticipation of actually grasping it.

E₁₀: **Removes obstruction in order to obtain a desired object.**

Location: Same as in E₄.

Object: Any object that the child shows interest in playing with and a barrier (e.g., pillow, Plexiglas, shoe box) that can be ed as an obstruction.

Directions: Gain the child's attention to an object he/she has shown interest in. While the child is attending to the object, place it behind a barrier, but have it remain *totally* visible and close enough so that the child can easily reach it.

Response: Child pushes or removes the barrier to gain direct access to the object, or reaches and/or moves around (over) the barrier to obtain the toy.

E₁₁: **Does not pull either of two supports when an object is placed between them.**

Location: Same as in E₄.

Object: Any object that the child shows interest in playing with and two supports (e.g., cloths) about 18 inches × 8 inches.

Directions: Place the two supports on a table surface in front of the child about 8 inches apart with each support about 8 inches from the child. Place a toy the child desires on one of the supports so that he/she must pull the cloth in order to obtain the toy. Repeat several times, placing the toy on one support, then the other. Following several presentations, place the object between the two supports where the child can clearly see it is not resting on the cloths.

Response: The child ignores the supports and tries to reach the toy directly, or simply does not attempt to obtain the toy. To ascertain that the child has not lost interest in obtaining the toy, place the object on one of the two supports to see if he/she will again retrieve the toy.

E₁₂: **Pulls the correct one of two strings in order to obtain a toy attached to one.**

Location: Same as in E₄, or seated in a high chair that is placed up against a table, or seated on the parent's lap at a table.

Object: Any object of interest to the child and two heavy-duty pieces of cord 30 to 36 inches in length.

Directions: Attach an object to one of the strings and place it 2 to 3 feet away from the child. Then, extend both strings simultaneously toward the child, with the strings about 6 to 8 inches apart. Repeat several times, alternating the side to which the object is presented.

Response: During each trial presentation, the child pulls *only* the string to which the object is attached. However, if the child begins to pull the incorrect string, notices the error, and corrects his/her mistake, the child is credited with successful retrieval. Pulling both strings simultaneously is scored as a failure.

E_{13}: **Uses "T" stick as a tool to obtain a desired object that is out of reach.**

Location: Same as in E_4 or seated in a high chair that is placed up against a table, or seated on the parent's lap at a table.

Object: Any toy of interest to the child and a "T" stick. The stick should be 15 to 18 inches in length with a 6-inch piece of wood (the same diameter as the stick) attached to one end so as to make a "T"-shaped instrument.

Directions: Place an object about 18 to 20 inches away from the child with the "T" stick placed next to the toy, about 6 inches away from it. The body of the "T" stick should be extended toward the child and be within reach. If the child does not spontaneously use the stick to obtain the object, the examiner may demonstrate the use of the stick as a tool.

Response: Child obtains the toy using the stick as a tool either spontaneously or following a demonstration.

E_{14}: **Removes objects placed in a small matchbox.**

Location: Same as in E_4.

Object: Any number of small objects of interest to the child and a small matchbox about 5 inches long and 3 inches wide.

Directions: Show the child both the small objects and the matchbox (which is opened). With the child watching, insert the objects into the matchbox, close it, but leave it open about $\frac{1}{4}$ inch on one side. Hand the matchbox to the child with the closed side toward him or her, encouraging the child to obtain the contents.

Response: Child turns matchbox around and inserts finger into the small opening to pull the matchbox open, or pushes the matchbox open from the closed side.

E_{15}: **Invents method to place a necklace into a container.**

Location: Same as in E_4.

Object: A long necklace and a container (e.g., a plastic measuring cup) that is narrow at the bottom and widens at the top.

Directions: See Uzgiris and Hunt, pp. 173–174.

Response: Child invents a method to place the necklace into the container but without showing foresight initially. That is, following several unsuccessful attempts, the child, by trial and error, succeeds in inserting the necklace into the container.

E₁₆: **Avoids attempt to stack solid ring following an unsuccessful attempt.**

Location: Same as in E₄.

Object: A set of five or six plastic or wooden stacking rings, one of which has been made solid by filling the hole, and a stick on which to place the rings.

Directions: See Uzgiris and Hunt, pp. 174–175.

Response: Child attempts to stack the solid ring and avoids it subsequently; or, each time the solid ring is encountered, he/she attempts to stack it, but noticing no hole, places it off to one side.

E₁₇: **Shows foresight in placing a small chain into a matchbox.**

Location: Same as in E₄.

Object: A small matchbox about 5 inches long and 3 inches wide and a small chain or necklace 10 to 12 inches in diameter.

Directions: Without the child watching, place the chain into the matchbox, which should be left about half open. Show the child the chain inside the container; then, without him/her watching, remove the chain and place both it and the matchbox on the table in front of the child with the chain spread out. Encourage the child to put the chain into the matchbox.

Response: Child adopts a method that takes into account the size of the container opening and the shape of the chain from the first attempt. Generally, the chain is either "bunched-up" or held high above the container, and inserted into the matchbox.

E₁₈: **Uses stick to push out the contents of a *clear* plastic tube.**

Location: Same as in E₄.

Object: A stick about 8 to 10 inches long and a clear plastic tube about 5 inches long and 1 inch in diameter.

Directions: Without the child watching, insert a small plastic animal, squeeze toy, yarn doll, or other small pliable object in the center of the tube. Show the child the tube and call his/her attention to the object inside. The tube should then be placed vertically in front of the child so it "stands up," with the stick placed in front of, and perpendicular to the tube between it and the child. Encourage the child to get the toy out.

Response: Child uses the stick to push out the contents of the tube. The child may first try to get the toy by reaching in, but finds that he/she cannot reach it, and then uses the stick.

E₁₉: **Uses stick to push out the contents of an *opaque* tube.**

Location: Same as in E₄.

Object: A stick about 8 to 10 inches long and an opaque tube about 5 inches long and 1 inch in diameter.

Directions: Same as in E_{18}.

Response: Child uses the stick to push out the contents of the tube.

IIIA: VOCAL IMITATION

E_{20}:   **Responds to voice.**

Location: Same as in E_1, or any position comfortable to the child.

Object: None.

Directions: While outside the child's visual field, either to the side or behind the child, talk to him/her in a soft, pleasant tone. Repeat several times if necessary.

Response: Child turns head, vocalizes, shifts activity level, changes facial expression, or otherwise indicates that he/she is attending to the examiner's voice.

E_{21}:   **Vocalizes similar sounds in response to cooing sounds.**

Location: Any position comfortable to the child.

Object: None.

Directions: See Uzgiris and Hunt, pp. 177–178.

Response: Child vocalizes similar sounds in response to the examiner's production of cooing sounds.

E_{22}:   **Imitates cooing sounds.**

Location: Any position comfortable to the child.

Object: None.

Directions: See Uzgiris and Hunt, pp. 177–178.

Response: Child vocalizes similar sounds in response to the examiner's production of cooing sounds and shifts to match those of the examiner, or imitates the cooing sounds immediately.

E_{23}:   **Vocalizes similar sounds in response to familiar words.**

Location: Any position comfortable to the child.

Object: None, or an object whose name the examiner is attempting to elicit. (See vocal imitation scale materials—Appendix C.)

Directions: See Uzgiris and Hunt, pp. 179–180.

Response: Vocalizes similar sounds in response to the familiar words produced by the examiner, but does not shift to match those of the examiner.

E_{24}:   **Imitates one novel word.**

Location: Any position comfortable to the child.

Object: None, or any object that the examiner is attempting to have the child name.

Directions: See Uzgiris and Hunt, pp. 181–182.

Response: Child imitates one novel word produced by the examiner directly.

E_{25}:   **Imitates two novel words.**

Location: Any position comfortable to the child.

Object: None, or several different objects that the examiner is attempting to have the child name.

Directions: See Uzgiris and Hunt, pp. 181–182.

Response: Child imitates two novel words produced by the examiner directly.

IIIB: GESTURAL IMITATION

E₂₆: Attends to gestures performed by the examiner.

Location: Any position comfortable to the child.

Object: Several different toys and materials that can be used to perform both simple and complex gestures familiar to the child.

Directions: While the child is both not actively playing with any toys and attending to the examiner, the examiner should perform a gesture that is familiar to the child (e.g., tapping on a roly-poly). Repeat the gesture several times, occasionally performing a different gesture (e.g., clapping the hands).

Response: Child attends to at least two different gestures. Generally, each time the examiner performs a gesture, the child ceases what he/she is doing and watches the behavior the examiner is performing.

E₂₇: Imitates simple gestures by gradual approximation.

Location: Any position comfortable to the child.

Object: Several different toys and materials that can be used to perform familiar simple gestures.

Directions: See Uzgiris and Hunt, p. 182.

Response: The child imitates the modeled actions by gradual approximation. That is, on each successive presentation by the examiner, the child more closely imitates the gesture, finally imitating the action

several times; or, during any one attempt at imitation, the child comes closer to imitating the action, finally imitating the action successfully.

E₂₈: Imitates invisible gestures with an object by gradual approximation.

Location: Any position comfortable to the child.

Object: Any small object that the child can easily hold in his/her hand.

Directions: While the child is attentive, model a gesture that the child is unable to observe him/herself perform (e.g., putting a block on the head, placing beads behind the neck). To be sure the gestures used are unfamiliar, question the parent(s) to ascertain whether the gestures have been taught or frequently demonstrated to the child. Repeat the unfamiliar gestures several times and pause to observe the child's response.

Response: The child imitates the unfamiliar, invisible gesture by gradual approximation.

E₂₉: Imitates an unfamiliar, invisible gesture without an object by gradual approximation.

Location: Any position comfortable to the child.

Object: None.

Directions: See Uzgiris and Hunt, p. 185. (See also p. 19 of this manual.)

Response: The child imitates one unfamiliar, invisible gesture by gradual approximation.

E₃₀: **Imitates one unfamiliar, invisible gesture with an object.**

Location: Any position comfortable to the child.

Object: Same as in E₂₈.

Directions: Same as in E₂₈.

Response: Child immediately imitates one unfamiliar, invisible gesture using an object.

E₃₁: **Imitates two unfamiliar, invisible gestures with objects.**

Location: Any position comfortable to the child.

Object: Same as in E₂₈.

Directions: Same as in E₂₈.

Response: The child immediately imitates two unfamiliar, invisible gestures using objects.

E₃₂: **Imitates two unfamiliar, invisible gestures without objects.**

Location: Any position comfortable to the child.

Object: None.

Directions: See Uzgiris and Hunt, p. 185.

Response: The child immediately imitates two unfamiliar, invisible gestures without using any objects.

E₃₃: **Imitates three unfamiliar, invisible gestures with objects.**

Location: Any position comfortable to the child.

Object: Same as in E₂₈.

Directions: Same as in E₂₈.

Response: The child immediately imitates three unfamiliar, invisible gestures using objects.

IV: OPERATIONAL CAUSALITY

E₃₄: **Vocalizes and/or smiles in response to adult talking.**

Location: Same as in E₁, or any position comfortable to the child.

Object: None.

Directions: While the child is quiet and alert, lean over him/her, and attract his/her attention. Talk to the child in a soft, pleasant voice. Repeat several times if necessary.

Response: Child vocalizes, laughs, and/or smiles in response to the adult talking to him/her.

E₃₅: **Pushes or pulls an adult's hand as a causal action to have a behavior instigated or repeated.**

Location: Any situation during the assessment period.

Object: None.

Directions: Generally, this behavior occurs spontaneously during the assessment period, and is not elicited as part of the test situation. Often, the child will take the parent's hand and pull or push it toward something the child desires or to have a behavior performed. In some instances, the child attempts to direct the parent's hand and arm toward the location where the child desires to go, or toward an object the child wants.

Response: Child attempts to engage the adult into a goal-directed sequence by taking his/her hand and directing it toward the desired goal.

E₃₆: Child repeats behavior (shows off) to maintain an adult's attention.

Location: Any situation during the assessment period.

Object: None.

Directions: Generally, this behavior occurs spontaneously during the assessment period, and is usually elicited in response to the examiner's and/or parent's social responses (smiling, laughing, talking) to something the child says or does. If the behavior does not occur spontaneously, the examiner can often elicit the response by making a "big deal" of something the child does or says (e.g., playing pat-a-cake).

Response: Child repeats behavior that the examiner and/or parent has reinforced to maintain the adult's attention.

F₃₇: Uses gesture *plus* visual/vocal behaviors to have an adult instigate a desired action, get something the child desires, or otherwise attempt to communicate to an adult.

Location: Any situation during the assessment period.

Object: None.

Directions: Generally, this behavior occurs spontaneously during the assessment period.

The child may use pointing, a "come here" gesture, or any other communicative gesture to gain the examiner's and/or parent's attention. However, the gesture must be accompanied by *both* visually looking at the person the child is attempting to communicate to with a concomitant vocal utterance as part of the communicative act.

Response: Child uses a gesture plus visual/vocal behaviors as a communicative act. The child either looks at the person he/she is attempting to communicate to or looks back and forth between the person and the object or event to which the child is attempting to call the person's attention. The vocalization used does not have to be a socially recognized word, but can be any vocal pattern that apparently is used as part of the communicative act.

V: CONSTRUCTION OF OBJECTS IN SPACE

E₃₈: Searches for sound with eyes.

Location: Same as in E₁, or any position comfortable to the child.

Object: A sound producing object such as a rattle, a bell, or a squeak toy.

Directions: While outside the child's visual field, the examiner shakes a rattle or other sound-producing object gently to either the child's left or right side, and slightly behind the child so he/she cannot see the object. Repeat several times with a 5- to

10-second pause between presentations. Present at least two trials to both the child's left and right sides.

Response: Child turns his/her eyes (but may not turn the head) to the side the sound is presented on at least two occasions.

E₃₉: **Turns mirror over to view functional side.**

Location: Any position comfortable to the child where both hands are free to manipulate the mirror (see also E₄).

Object: A small pocket mirror (with no handle) about 5 inches long and 3 inches wide.

Directions: Show the child his/her reflection in the mirror, holding it about 10 to 12 inches from his/her face. Once the child has focused on his/her reflection, turn the mirror around and offer it to the child with the functional side facing away from the child.

Response: Child grasps the mirror and turns it around to again view his/her reflection.

E₄₀: **Turns picture over to view functional side.**

Location: Any position comfortable to the child where both hands are free to manipulate the materials.

Object: Any picture, photograph, greeting card, etc. about 5 inches long and 3 inches wide that has a blank reverse side.

Directions: Show the child the picture, holding it about 10 to 12 inches from his/her face. Once the child is attending to the pic-ture, turn it around and offer it to the child with the functional side facing away.

Response: Child grasps the picture and turns it around to again view the functional side.

E₄₁: **Places (drops) objects into a container.**

Location: Same as in E₄₀.

Object: A cup and five or six 1-inch wooden cubes or other similarly sized objects (e.g., stringing beads).

Directions: See Uzgiris and Hunt, p. 196.

Response: Child places or drops at least two objects into the container.

E₄₂: **Stirs with a spoon in a cup.**

Location: Same as in E₄₀.

Object: A cup and an adult-size spoon.

Directions: Demonstrate for the child the action of stirring with the spoon inside the cup. Place the cup in front of the child with the spoon next to it. Encourage the child to put the spoon in the cup.

Response: Child picks up the spoon and places it in the cup, although he/she may not imitate the stirring action. It is, however, necessary that the child purposefully insert the spoon inside the cup and not simply bang on it.

E₄₃: **Picks up stick to play xylophone.**

Location: Same as in E₄₀.

Object: Small toy xylophone and xylophone hammer.

Directions: Place the xylophone in front of the child and demonstrate hitting the toy. After several presentations, place the xylophone hammer next to the xylophone but at least 8 inches away from the toy. On each subsequent presentation, vary the positions where both the xylophone and hammer are placed.

Response: Child picks up the xylophone hammer and uses it to play the xylophone.

E₄₄: Bangs spoon on an inverted cup.

Location: Same as in E₄₀.

Object: A plastic cup and an adult-size spoon.

Directions: Place the cup upside down in front of the child and demonstrate banging on the cup with the spoon. After several presentations, place the spoon next to the cup but at least 8 inches away from it. On each subsequent presentation, vary the positions where both the cup and spoon are placed.

Response: Child picks up the spoon and bangs it on the inverted cup.

E₄₅: Dumps objects out of a narrow-necked container.

Location: Same as in E₄₀.

Object: A clear plastic bottle about 4 inches high and 1 inch in diameter, and several raisins.

Directions: Show the child both the container and the raisins. Without the child watching, place the raisins into the container and give the bottle to him/her. Encourage the child to remove the contents.

Response: Child purposefully removes the raisins by turning the container over to obtain them. Attempting to remove the contents by "drinking" or shaking the bottle does not receive credit as a correct response.

E₄₆: Places rings on a stacking stick.

Location: Same as in E₄₀.

Object: A set of five or six wooden stacking rings and a stick on which to place the rings.

Directions: Demonstrate to the child both placing the rings on the stick and removing them one at a time. Place the rings next to the child and, while holding the stacking stick, encourage the child to place the rings on the stick.

Response: Child places at least two rings on the stacking stick.

E₄₇: Makes a complex detour to obtain a desired object.

Note: The directions for scale step 11a on the Uzgiris and Hunt scales does not specify the type of detour that is to be traversed by the child in order to obtain an object made to come to rest on the far side of a detour barrier. Experience has found that the ability to make a detour around a simple barrier (e.g., a chair) is generally manifested much earlier than detours around complex barriers. Item E₄₇ was added to provide a measure for the latter type of ability.

Location: A cul-de-sac made by arranging chairs, tables, etc. in a U-shaped formation.

Object:	Any object of interest to the child that can be made to roll or move under the bottom part of the U-shaped cul-de-sac and come to rest on the other side.
Directions:	Begin playing a game with the child in the cul-de-sac. Preferably, the child should be positioned at the bottom of the U formation. While engaging in a play activity (e.g., rolling a ball back and forth), make the object pass under or over the cul-de-sac and come to rest out of reach on the other side.
Response:	Child looks at the object, and moves around the cul-de-sac to retrieve it. He/she may first attempt to reach for it, but realizes it is not accessible, and then moves around the barrier to get the toy.

VI: SCHEMES FOR RELATING TO OBJECTS

E$_{48}$: **Grasps examiner's finger.**

Location:	Any position comfortable to the child, although it is generally best to have the child supine on the floor or in a crib, or in an infant seat.
Object:	None.
Directions:	Gently insert your little finger into the child's palm. Then, move your finger gently from side to side, pulling slightly to elicit the grasping response. Repeat several times to both of the child's hands.
Response:	Child closes his/her fingers around the examiner's finger and holds on for 3 to 5 seconds.

E$_{49}$: **Child retains an object placed in the hand.**

Location:	Same as in E$_{48}$.
Object:	A rattle with an elongated handle, or any object with a diameter of ½ inch or less.
Directions:	While the child's hand is open, place the object into the palm, gently moving the object around to get the child to close his/her fingers around it. Repeat several times to both of the child's hands.
Response:	Child retains the object for 10 to 15 seconds.

E$_{50}$: **Drops or throws objects—no visual monitoring of the action.**

Note:	E$_{50}$ was added to the item pool of this scale to enable the examiner to discriminate between "letting go" actions that are exploratory in nature (scale step 7) and those simply involving abandonment of objects—usually in response to the examiner's attempt to elicit a critical behavior.
Location:	Any situation during the assessment.
Object:	None.
Directions:	The examiner does not attempt to elicit this response. It is generally observed during the course of the assessment.
Response:	Child throws, drops, or "flings" objects with no apparent interest in the effects of the actions.

E$_{51}$: **Socially instigated actions—self and/or others.**

Location:	Any position comfortable to the child.

Object:	Several different objects that tend to elicit socially instigated actions (see Appendix C—schemes scale materials).
Directions:	These behaviors are not specifically assessed, but generally occur spontaneously during the assessment period when the child is given the opportunity to play with materials that tend to elicit socially instigated actions.
Response:	Child manifests at least three different socially instigated actions on him/herself or on an adult (e.g., giving a drink, combing the hair, wiping the nose).

E₅₂: **Gives object to adult to instigate social interaction.**

Location:	Any position comfortable to the child.
Object:	None.
Directions:	Generally, this behavior occurs spontaneously during the course of the assessment. It is an attempt by the child to gain the attention of an adult or to otherwise instigate social interactions. Most often, the child deposits an object on the adult's lap (e.g., a ball) and waits for the adult's response.
Response:	Child gives an object to another person as an apparent attempt to instigate a social exchange.

E₅₃: **Engages in symbolic play.**

Location:	Any situation during the assessment.
Object:	Several different objects (e.g., a hexagonal nesting cup) that can be used as the *signifier* for other objects—the signified (e.g., a drinking cup).
Directions:	Generally, symbolic behaviors are manifested spontaneously during the course of the assessment if the child is capable of understanding the relationship between the signifier and the signified. However, the examiner can attempt to elicit symbolic behaviors if they are not observed incidentally. From among the different socially instigated behaviors manifested by the child (scale steps E₅₁ and 8), choose several in which signifier objects can be substituted for objects that the child has demonstrated the ability to use functionally (e.g., a toy rake for a comb) to enact behavioral responses. With the signified object (toy rake) within view, ask the child to "comb mommy's hair," and pause to observe the child's response. Present several *signified* objects in this manner, but do not suggest that the child use an object as a substitute for another.
Response:	Child manifests at least two symbolic behaviors either spontaneously or in response to the examiner's attempt to elicit the behaviors.

appendix C

SUGGESTED ASSESSMENT MATERIALS AND EQUIPMENT

The flexibility in administering the Uzgiris and Hunt scales permits the examiner to use various materials and equipment to assess a child's sensorimotor capabilities. Therefore, the materials listed should be considered suggestions only, and the examiner should feel free to substitute and/or add materials that enhance the elicitation of the critical behaviors. However, care should be taken to ensure that the procedures for administration of the assessment items are not changed as a function of the test materials used.

The abbreviations for the scales are as follows: OP—visual pursuit and the permanence of objects; ME—means for obtaining desired environmental events; VI—development of vocal imitation; GI—development of gestural imitation; OC—development of operational causality; SR—construction of objects in space; and SO—schemes for relating to objects. Materials that are used and/or are of utility in the administration of particular scales are so indicated by either an upper or lower case x. The upper case X indicates that the materials are specifically needed or are of primary utility in administration of one or more items on that scale. The lower case x indicates that the examiner may find the materials of some utility in the administration of one or more scale items. All of the materials suggested for the administration of the vocal imitation scale have been marked with a lower case x, and this indicates that the materials may be ones that the examiner can use to elicit either naming of the objects, or actions or sound patterns associated with the materials (i.e., familiar words, unfamiliar sound patterns, and unfamiliar words).

Materials	Description	Scale						
		OP	ME	VI	GI	OC	SR	SO
Roly-poly	A small roly-poly toy shaped like a clown that makes a noise when moved	X	X		x	X		X
Pop-beads	Eighteen multicolored plastic pop-beads made to form a large ring	X			x	x	X	X
Cord	Two pieces of heavy-duty cord each three feet in length	X	X					
Screens	Three cloth screens 18 inches × 18 inches. Each should be opaque and drab in color (e.g., gray)	X	X					X
Box	A plain brown cardboard box about 5 inches long by 4 inches wide by 4 inches deep	X					x	x
Rattles	Several different-size rattles—one shaped like a barbell, and another with a long, narrow handle		X		X		X	X
Blocks	Twelve multicolored 1-inch wooden counting cubes		X	x	X	x	X	X
Barriers	Several different barriers (e.g., a piece of clear Plexiglas 12 inches × 8 inches, a small pillow 12 inches × 12 inches, a shoe box)	x	X					X
T stick	A dowel stick 18 inches long and ½ inch in diameter with a 6 inch × ½ inch diameter piece of stick attached to one end so as to make it a "T"-shaped instrument		X					x
Sticks	Two dowel sticks—one 18 inches long and ½ inch in diameter, and one 10 inches by ¼ inch in diameter		X					x
Matchbox	A small matchbox about 5 inches long and 3 inches wide		X				x	x
Necklace	A long multicolored necklace made of small plastic or wooden beads		X		x	x		x
Container	A tall plastic container about 6 inches high that is narrow at the bottom and widens at the top		X				x	x
Stacking rings	A set of five or six plastic or wooden stacking rings, one of which has been made solid by filling the hole; and a stacking stick		X				X	x
Chain	A small chain or necklace about 10 to 12 inches in diameter that can be held in the palm of a small child's hand when bunched up		X		x			x
Clear plastic tube	A clear plastic tube, open at both ends, about 5 inches long and 1 inch in diameter		X					x

Materials	Description	Scale						
		OP	ME	VI	GI	OC	SR	SO
Opaque tube	An opaque plastic or cardboard tube, open at both ends, about 5 inches long and 1 inch in diameter		X					x
Squeeze toys	Several different squeeze toys shaped like animals that are pliable and produce a squeak when touched	x	x		X	x	x	X
Spoons	Four spoons—adult size (2), child size, and doll size	x	x		X	x	X	X
Slinky	A multicolored plastic Slinky		x		X	X		x
Paper	Several pieces of light-bond typing paper				X			X
String toys	Several different toys with movable joints, in the shapes of people or animals, which are moved (activated) by pulling a string	x				X		x
Pull toy	A small string-activated toy that produces some type of auditory feedback (e.g., music) when pulled					X		x
Pinwheel	A plastic pinwheel attached to a short stick that can be made to twirl when moved					X		x
Wind-up toys	Several different toys that move when activated by a wind-up mechanism. Preferably, the keys operating the toys should be unobtrusive					X		
Bell	A small hand bell with a handle about 4 inches long	x	x		X	x	X	X
Checkerboard cards	Two 4 inch × 4 inch checkerboard cards with ½-inch squares—one yellow and red, the other yellow and blue					X		
Plastic flowers	Several different artificial flowers that are attractive to the child			x			X	X
Mirror (nonbreakable)	A small pocket mirror (with no handle) about 5 inches long and 3 inches wide				x		X	x
Pictures	Several different pictures, photographs, greeting cards, etc. about 5 inches long and 3 inches wide, and that have blank reverse sides			x			X	x
Plastic animals	Several different-size plastic animals that the child is likely to be familiar with (e.g., barnyard animals)			x			X	x
Plastic human figures	Several different hard plastic lifelike human figures about 3 to 4 inches high			x			X	X
Finger puppets	Several different plastic finger puppets of characters the child is likely to be familiar with (e.g., Mickey Mouse, Snoopy, the Cookie Monster)			x	x	x	X	X

| | | Scale | | | | | | |
Materials	Description	OP	ME	VI	GI	OC	SR	SO
Cup	A small plastic cup about 4 inches high with a handle			x	x		X	X
Xylophone	A small toy xylophone about 4 inches long with a hammer					x	X	X
Small container	A small clear plastic narrow-necked container about 4 inches high and 1 inch in diameter						X	X
Clipboard	A clipboard 12 inches long and 9 inches wide that can be used as an incline when turned over		X				X	
Walking toy	A small plastic or wooden toy that moves by itself when placed on an incline						X	
Balls	Several different-size small rubber balls			x	x	x	X	X
Cars	Several different-size small cars—one that is friction operated, and another than rolls easily down an incline			x	x	X	X	X
Cotton	A large ball of cotton				x		x	X
Aluminum foil	Several different pieces of aluminum foil about 6 inches by 6 inches in size				X		x	X
Dolls	Several different-size dolls—one about 3 inches high made of pliable plastic, and one about 6 to 8 inches high, dressed appropriately (shirt, pants, shoes, etc.), that has hair that can be brushed	x		x			X	X
Bottles	A small plastic nursing bottle with a nipple, and a small plastic baby bottle designed for use in "feeding" a doll			x			X	X
Shoes	A small child-size shoe and a small doll-size shoe			x				X
Diaper	A small diaper designed to be used on a doll			x				X
Hats	A child-size hat and a doll-size hat			x				X
Socks	A child-size sock and a doll-size sock			x				X
Pan	A doll-size pan with a lid			x			x	X
Plates	Several different-size doll plates			x				X
Bowl	A small plastic cereal bowl			x			x	X
Straws	Several plastic or paper straws			x				X

Materials	Description	Scale						
		OP	ME	VI	GI	OC	SR	SO
Bibs	A child-size bib and a doll-size bib			x				X
Hair brushes	An adult-size hair brush and a doll-size hair brush							X
Combs	An adult-size comb and a doll-size comb			x				X
Washcloth	A small washcloth or sponge							X
Soap	A small bar of soap, the size usually provided by motels							X
Toothbrush	A small toothbrush and a small tube of toothpaste							X
Kleenex	A small box of Kleenex							X
Band-Aids	Several different-size Band-Aids, bandages, and gauze							X
Raisins	A small box of raisins						X	X
Cereal	A small box of dry cereal						X	X

VALIDITY OF SCORING PROCEDURES FOR QUANTIFYING THE SENSORIMOTOR PERFORMANCE OF INFANTS AS MEASURED BY THE UZGURIS AND HUNT SCALES

The concurrent validity of the estimated developmental age (EDA) placements assigned to each of the landmarks comprising the content of the Uzgiris and Hunt scales, and of the scores derived using the EDAs, was examined in a study of 36 handicapped and at-risk infants and toddlers administered both the Uzgiris and Hunt (1975) Scales and the Griffiths (1954) Mental Development Scales. Both scales were administered to the subjects as part of their participation in a model mother-infant intervention program (Dunst, 1975). The administration of the scales occurred independent of the purposes of the present study.

The distribution of the subjects (19 girls and 17 boys) according to diagnosis, chronological age, mental age, and general intelligence quotient (Griffiths, 1954) is presented in Table 1. The mean chronological age of the subjects was 14.42 months (SD = 7.36). The subjects' mean mental age was 9.04 months (SD = 5.44). The group's mean general intelligence quotient (GQ) was 77.25 (SD = 17.40). The families of the subjects covered the entire socioeconomic range, although the majority were from middle- to middle upper-class backgrounds. All but one subject resided in a household where both the mother and father were present. The families were all from the metropolitan Washington, D.C., area at the time the children were tested.

The quantitative *developmental performance* of each subject on the Uzgiris and Hunt scales was determined in two ways. First, each subject was assigned a score equal to the EDA placement corresponding to the highest item passed on each of the separate scales (see Appendix A). Thus, each subject received an EDA score for object permanence, means-ends abilities, vocal imitation, gestural imitation, causality, spatial relationships, and schemes for relating to objects. Second, an estimated mental age (EMA) was determined for each subject. This was computed as the average of the seven separate EDA scores.

Table 1. Chronological ages (CA), mental ages (MA), and general intelligence quotients (GQ) for a group of handicapped and at-risk infants and toddlers

Diagnosis	CA (months)				MA (months)				GQ			
	0–6	7–12	13–18	19–30	0–6	7–12	13–18	19–24	45–63	64–75	76–87	88–105
Down's syndrome	3	5	2	2	6	6	0	0	3	3	4	2
Brain damage	0	0	2	4	0	2	2	2	1	1	3	1
Spina bifida	0	1	2	2	1	3	0	1	0	1	3	1
At-risk[a]	3	2	0	0	3	1	1	0	0	0	0	5
Cerebral palsy	0	1	1	2	1	1	1	1	1	3	0	0
Mental retardation[b]	0	0	1	3	1	1	1	1	2	2	0	0

[a]Included three infants from lower socioeconomic backgrounds considered at-risk for developmental retardation and two infants identified as "neglected" according to local Department of Social Services criteria.

[b]Due to unknown causes.

The quantitative developmental performance of each subject on the Griffiths scales was determined in a similar manner. First, each subject received a developmental age score for each scale on the Griffiths test (locomotor, personal-social, hearing and speech, eye-hand coordination, and performance). Second, an overall mental age was determined. The developmental ages for the individual scales and the overall mental age were determined according to the scoring methods described by Griffiths (1954).

In addition to determining the subject's quantitative performance levels on both the Uzgiris and Hunt and Griffiths scales, *deviation scores* were also derived. For the Griffiths scale, this consisted of computing developmental quotients (DQs) for each scale included on the test, and computing a GQ based on the child's overall performance. The method for deriving these deviation scores is the standard mental age/chronological age multiplied by 100 (Griffiths, 1954).

Eight separate deviation scores were computed for each subject based on their performance on the Uzgiris and Hunt scales. First, individual deviation scores were determined for the seven separate sensorimotor domains. A deviation score was computed by subtracting a child's EDA placement from his or her chronological age. Second, an average deviation (AD) score was determined for each subject. The AD score was computed as the mean of the seven separate scale deviation scores. Deviation scores were intended to provide a measure of the extent to which discrepancies in sensorimotor development were present.

The means and SDs for both the developmental performance scores and the deviation scores on the Uzgiris and Hunt and Griffiths scales are shown in Table 2. Two major types of data analysis were performed. First, product-movement correlations were computed between the developmental performance scores on both the Uzgiris and Hunt scales and the Griffiths scales. Second, product-movement correlations were computed between the deviation scores on both the Uzgiris and Hunt and Griffiths scales.

Table 3 presents the analysis for the quantitative performance scores. As can be seen, the performance scores on the Uzgiris and Hunt scales and the Griffiths scales correlate significantly both within and across scales. In terms of concurrent validity, these results reveal that the EDAs are good indicators of a child's actual quantitative developmental performance. The high correlation between *actual* MAs and *estimated* MAs indicates further that the procedure for determining a child's overall quantitative level of developmental performance is a valid one. Even with chronological age (CA) partialled out, the correlation between mental age (MA) and EMA remained high [r (34) = 0.83, $P < 0.01$, two-tailed test].

The actual relationship between the MA and EMA scores is graphically depicted in Figure 1. Examination of Figure 1 reveals several things. First, the procedure for determining EMAs generally underestimates a child's actual MA. However, the difference between the mean MA and EMA scores (see Table 2) was found not to be significant as determined by a correlated samples t test, [t (35) = 0.28, n.s.]. Second, EMAs appear to be better estimators for children

Table 2. Means and standard deviations (SDs) on the Uzgiris and Hunt scales and Griffiths scales for both the performance and deviation scores

Scales	Developmental performance scores		Deviation scores[a]	
	Mean	SD	Mean	SD
Uzgiris and Hunt scales				
Object permanence	8.33	5.60	14.00	3.40
Means-ends abilities	9.64	4.35	15.31	4.46
Vocal imitation	7.83	6.18	13.53	5.41
Gestural imitation	9.81	5.76	15.47	4.75
Causality	9.08	5.12	14.75	3.84
Spatial relationships	9.67	4.63	15.33	3.90
Schemes	8.94	4.65	14.67	4.78
Estimated mental age	9.04	4.73	—	—
Average deviation score	—	—	14.72	3.66
Griffiths Scales				
Locomotor	10.91	5.47	79.81	22.19
Personal-social	10.54	5.46	76.03	20.55
Hearing and speech	9.90	5.55	71.67	20.37
Eye-hand coordination	10.93	5.85	77.33	16.27
Performance	10.61	5.63	74.83	13.99
Mental age	10.71	5.44	—	—
General intelligence quotient	—	—	77.25	17.40

[a]A constant of 20 was added to the deviation scores on the Uzgiris and Hunt scales to eliminate negative scores.

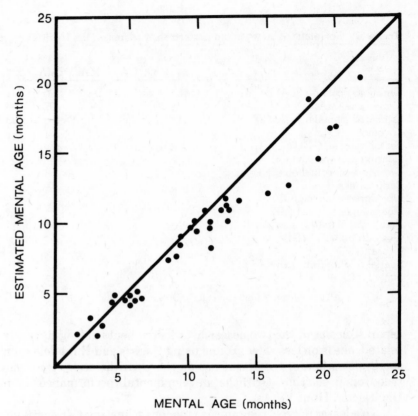

Figure 1. Scatter plot of actual and of estimated mental ages as measured, respectively, by the Griffiths scales and Uzgiris and Hunt scales.

developmentally under 12 months of age. A regression analysis predicting *actual* MAs from EMAs yielded the equation $MA = 0.68 + 1.11 \times EMA$, with a standard error of estimate of 1.32 months. Thus, EMAs underestimate actual MAs, on the average, by about 1.75 months.

Table 4 presents the analysis for the deviation scores. Several things are revealed by these results. First, on the Griffiths scales, both the individual scale DQs and the overall GQ correlate significantly with each other. Second, on the Uzgiris and Hunt scales, both the individual scale deviation scores and the AD scores correlate significantly with each other. Thus, in terms of within-scale relationships, deviation scores, whether computed as DQs or deviations from CA, are good predictors of one another. Of particular significance are the findings that the GQ and AD scores, respectively, correlate substantially with the deviation scores of the individual scales

on the Griffiths and Uzgiris and Hunt assessment instruments. These results indicate that the average or overall indices of developmental delay are excellent predictors of individual scale deviations.

Comparisons between the Griffiths and the Uzgiris and Hunt scales revealed that, although all correlations were significant, the magnitude of the correlation coefficients was generally much lower than for the within-scale correlations. The average of the 35 correlation coefficients among the individual scales on the Griffiths and Uzgiris and Hunt tests was −0.46. This indicates that, on the average, only 21% of the variance in deviation scores on the Griffiths scales are estimated or predicted by the deviation scores on the Uzgiris and Hunt scales. Thus, although the deviation scores for the

Table 3. Correlations between the performance scores on the Uzgiris and Hunt scales and the Griffiths Mental Development scales

	CA	MA	EMA	LM	PS	HS	EH	PR	OP	ME	VI	GI	OC	SR	SO
				Griffiths scales					Uzgiris and Hunt scales						
Chronological age (CA)	—	0.91	.90	.91	.88	.83	.92	.92	.89	.82	.67	.75	.86	.89	.90
Mental age (MA)		—	.97	.96	.98	.96	.98	.98	.91	.87	.83	.88	.91	.88	.94
Estimated mental age (EMA)			—	.93	.97	.96	.95	.93	.93	.93	.87	.91	.91	.88	.94
Locomotor (LM)				—	.95	.89	.93	.93	.87	.83	.76	.86	.88	.84	.90
Personal-social (PS)					—	.97	.95	.95	.89	.88	.86	.88	.90	.86	.92
Hearing and speech (HS)						—	.92	.90	.86	.87	.91	.90	.87	.82	.91
Eye-hand coordination (EH)							—	.98	.92	.85	.77	.83	.89	.90	.93
Performance (PR)								—	.90	.83	.74	.81	.88	.88	.92
Object permanence (OP)									—	.85	.73	.84	.84	.84	.88
Means-ends abilities (ME)										—	.77	.82	.85	.83	.86
Vocal imitation (VI)											—	.84	.71	.71	.77
Gestural imitation (GI)												—	.79	.70	.81
Causality (OC)													—	.78	.91
Spatial relationships (SR)														—	.81
Schemes (SO)															—

NOTE: All correlations significant at the 0.01 level (two-tailed test).

separate scales of the two assessment instruments are significantly related, one is on less safer ground using Uzgiris and Hunt deviation scores as estimators of deviations on the Griffiths scales than was true for predicting Griffiths developmental performance from Uzgiris and Hunt EDAs.

To a lesser degree, the same is true for estimating GQ scores using the AD scores derived from the Uzgiris and Hunt scales as the predictor variable. The correlation between GQ and AD was −0.63. This indicated that 40% of the variance in GQ scores was accounted for by the AD scores. Therefore, the use of the AD scores as a predictor of GQ scores is much better than the average deviation scores for the separate Uzgiris and Hunt scales, but it is still not as good an estimator as was found for predicting *actual* MAs from EMAs.

To determine the validity of the procedure presented in Section 4 (p. 34) for determining whether discrepancies in sensorimotor development are present, a 3×3 chi-square analysis was performed using DQ scores (40 to 63, 64 to 65, and 76+)[1] versus ranges of deviation

scores (+4 to −4, 0 to −6, and −10 to −6) as the criterion measures. A subject was assigned to one of the three deviation categories if his or her scores on at least five out of seven of the individual scales fell within a particular range. The chi-square analysis was significant ($\chi^2 (4) = 10.04$, $P < 0.05$). The correlation between DQ and deviation categories was therefore also significant ($C = 0.47$, $P < 0.05$) (Siegel, 1956). The results indicated that the deviation scoring procedure was sensitive for determining group membership in each of the three DQ categories.

The results of the present investigation are quite consistent with previous studies that have reported significant relationships between sensorimotor abilities as measured by the Uzgiris and Hunt scales and psychometric test performance (Wachs, 1970; Wachs & DeRemer, 1978). Both the EDA scores assigned to each of the landmarks on the Uzgiris and Hunt scales and the scores derived using these age placements (EMA, individual scale deviation scores, and AD scores) were found to be significantly related to psychometric test performance as measured by the Griffiths Mental Development Scales. Therefore, it can be concluded that the methods presented in this clinical and educational manual for quantifying both sensori-

---

[1]The standard deviation on the Griffiths (1954) mental development scale is equal to 12.

Table 4. Correlations between the deviation scores on the Uzgiris and Hunt scales and the Griffiths Mental Development scales

	GQ	AD	Griffiths Scales LM	PS	HS	EH	PR	Uzgiris and Hunt Scales OP	ME	VI	GI	OC	SR	SO
General intelligence quotients (GQ)	—	−0.63	.90	.94	.88	.84	.86	−.51	−.48	−.60	−.61	−.62	−.42*	−.53
Average deviation score (AD)		—	−.52	−.57	−.65	−.50	−.48	.84	.93	.85	.87	.84	.82	.90
Locomotor (LM)			—	.83	.70	.66	.69	−.42*	−.38*	−.46	−.53	−.56	−.35*	−.46
Personal-social (PS)				—	.84	.69	.76	−.44	−.47	−.60	−.55	−.54	−.34*	−.47
Hearing and speech (HS)					—	.67	.66	−.47	−.51	−.73	−.65	−.59	−.38*	−.48
Eye-hand coordination (EH)						—	.88	−.43	−.36*	−.41*	−.48	−.51	−.40*	−.42*
Performance (PR)							—	−.42*	−.35*	−.41*	−.44	−.49	−.33*	−.44
Object permanence (OP)								—	.75	.59	.73	.64	.66	.73
Means-ends abilities (ME)									—	.70	.74	.80	.81	.84
Vocal imitation (VI)										—	.79	.60	.62	.69
Gestural imitation (GI)											—	.67	.56	.71
Causality (OC)												—	.63	.82
Spatial relationships (SR)													—	.71
Schemes (SO)														—

*$P < 0.05$ (two-tailed test); all remaining correlations are significant at the 0.01 level (two-tailed test).

motor performance levels and the extent to which there are discrepancies in development are valid procedures.

Despite the fact that the EMAs and their derivations have utility for the quantitative description of a child's sensorimotor performance, the shortcomings and limitations of these scores must be pointed out. Available evidence clearly indicates that the level of sensorimotor development at one age has little or no relationship to the level of performance at subsequent ages (King & Seegmiller, 1973; Lewis & McGurk, 1972; Uzgiris, 1973). In other words, EDAs, and consequently scores derived from them, have little or no predictive value. As Uzgiris (1976) has noted, sensorimotor progress is best characterized as a discontinuous developmental process that is more step-like than linear in nature. Therefore, EDA-derived scores would appear to have utility *only* for describing a child's current developmental standing, and the clinician should use them solely for this purpose.

The most apparent limitation of the procedures for quantifying a child's sensorimotor performance is that EDA-derived scores provide absolutely no information concerning either a child's actual sensorimotor capabilities or his or her patterns of sensorimotor performance. Moreover, quantitative data provide no basis for determining the types of experiences best adapted to foster developmental progress. Quantitative data have the utility of assessing only a limited aspect of a child's sensorimotor capabilities. The clinician should recognize this, and view the quantitative procedure described in this manual as a very small part of a more global clinical-educational process. If perceived as such, both the strengths and weaknesses of quantitative data are most likely to be apparent.

REFERENCES

Dunst, C. J. The Northern Virginia Parent-Infant Education Program. In C. J. Dunst (Ed.), *Trends in early intervention services—Methods, models, and evaluation.* Arlington, Virginia: Department of Human Resources, 1975.

Griffiths, R. *The abilities of babies.* London: University of London Press, 1954.

King, W., & Seegmiller, B. Performance of 14- to 22-month-old black, first-born male infants on two tests of cognitive development. *Developmental Psychology,* 1973, *8,* 317–326.

Lewis, M., & McGurk, H. Infant intelligence. *Science*, 1972, *178*, 1174–1176.

Siegel, J. *Nonparametric statistics for the behavioral sciences.* New York: McGraw-Hill, 1956.

Uzgiris, I. Patterns of cognitive development in infancy. *Merrill-Palmer Quarterly*, 1973, *19*, 181–204.

Uzgiris, I. Organization of sensorimotor intelligence. In M. Lewis (Ed.), *Origins of intelligence: Infancy and early childhood.* New York: Plenum Press, 1976.

Uzgiris, I., & Hunt, J. McV. *Assessment in infancy: Ordinal scales of psychological development.* Urbana: University of Illinois Press, 1975.

Wachs, T. Report on the utility of a Piaget-based infant scale with older retarded children. *Developmental Psychology*, 1970, *2*, 449.

Wachs, T., & DeRemer, P. Adaptive behavior and Uzgiris-Hunt scale performance of young, developmentally disabled children. *American Journal of Mental Deficiency*, 1978, *83*, 171–176.

Index

Operational causality
  guidelines for determining, 20–21
  types of causal behavior
    gives object, 21
    procedure, 20
    touches adult, 21
Operational causality scale
  actions used to elicit causality, 20
  administration of items on, 21
  experimental assessment item description, 85–86
  scoring of behaviors on, 21
Ordinal scales, 1
  and administration procedures, 3–4
  and ceiling level, 3
  differences between psychometric scales and, 3–4
  similarities with psychometric scales, 3–4
  utility of, 1, 7

P

Patterns of responses, scaling, *see* Scalogram analysis
Perceptual contingency level, *see* Phase Intervention model, Phase I
Phase Intervention model, 50–55
  Phase I, 50–51
    basic premise underlying, 51
    goals and objectives of, 50
    intervention activities, 51
  response class categories in, 50–51
  Phase III, 52–55
    goals and objectives of, 52
    intervention activities for, 52
    special considerations in implementing activities in, 55
  Phase II, 51–52
    behaviors to be attained in, 51–52
    goals and objectives of, 51
    intervention activities for, 52
Prepositional language, in Phase III intervention activities, 53
Product-movement correlations, 98
Profile of Abilities form, 27, 29, 31, 33, 67–76
Profile of abilities, uses for, 26
Profile of assessment results of sensorimotor abilities, 25–26
Psychoeducational needs, procedures for determining, 7, 30–36, 50–55
Psychometric tests and administration procedures, 3–4

Q

Qualitative characteristics of sensorimotor development
  determination of, 6–7
  uses for, 6

Quantitative characteristics of sensorimotor performance, 6

R

Receptive language, in Phase III intervention activities, 53
Record forms
  description of, 9–14
    critical action codes, 12
    critical behaviors attained, 13
    developmental stage placements, 11–12
    eliciting contexts, 12
    estimated developmental age (EDA) placements assigned, 10–11
    observation section, 14
    scale steps, 9–10
    scoring system, 13–14
    see also Summary record form
Recording assessment results of sensorimotor abilities
  inclusion of information on sensorimotor capabilities, 24–25
  procedure for summarizing individual scale record results, 24
  on Summary record form, 23–24
Reliability, interobserver, 5
Representational problem solving, in Phase III intervention activities, 53

Representational thought, 54

S

Scale steps, 9–10
Scalogram analysis, index of consistency (I) for, 4
  I values in
    in studies with nonretarded infants, 4
    in studies with retarded and handicapped infants, 5
Schemes for relating to objects scale
  administration of items on, 22
  experimental assessment item description, 89–90
  scoring of behaviors on, 22
Scoring of scales, *see* Administration of scales
Scoring system
  scoring categories, 13–14
  scoring symbols used in, 13–14
Semantic language activities, In Phase III intervention activities, 52, 53–54
Sensorimotor development
  patterns of
    in normal infants, 26–33
    in retarded and handicapped infants, 5
  qualitative characteristics of, 6–7
  quantitative characteristics of, 6

NOTES

NOTES

NOTES

NOTES

NOTES

NOTES

NOTES

NOTES